The First Degree Companion:

Articles and Advice for Beginners

by Taggart King

Copyright © 2023 Taggart King.

All rights reserved. No part of this book covered by the copyrights hereon may be reproduced or copied in any manner whatsoever without written permission.

www.reiki-evolution.co.uk

taggart@reiki-evolution.co.uk

Contents

About This Book 9
How to use this book 9
I want you to scribble in this book! 10

Fundamentals 11

Back to Basics: Reiki First Degree 13
Connecting to the energy 13
Developing your Sensitivity to the energy 15
Working on yourself 16
Treating other people 18
The Reiki Precepts 21
Finally 23

The Precepts 25
Usui's precepts aren't what is commonly taught in the West 26
Aren't negative affirmations a bad idea? 27
Stage One 28
Stage Two 28

Mindfulness and Compassion 29
Mindfulness 29
Compassion 30

How to start a Reiki treatment 33
A simple ritual to get your Reiki treatment started 33
Affirm 33
Connect 34
Build 34
Merge 34
Flow 35
Nice and simple 35
Over to you 36

What hand positions should I use? 37
Are there hand positions that you should always use? 37
Varying your hand positions for each client 37

How long should I spend in each hand position? . 39
Treat like clockwork? 39
Altering your treatments to suit the client 39
How to know how long to take in one position 40
Over to you 41

Do I need to keep at least one hand on a person when I treat them? 43

Keep touching or you'll lose the 'connection'? 43
What's the difference between hands-on and hands-off? 43
Basically Reiki is a hands-on practice 44
How are we connected? 44
Over to you 45

Reiki Sensations 47

Attunements or empowerments 47
Experiencing energy 48
Sensations experienced by people you treat 50
Summary 51

Treating both sides: is this necessary? 53

An unnecessary Reiki rule? 53
Could we just hold their hand for 60 minutes? 53
We don't just treat the square inches underneath our palms 54
Turning over routinely is so disruptive 55
Over to you 55

What if I get it wrong? 57

Getting anxious about our Reiki 57
Treatments that 'go wrong' 57
Reiki is above all that fiddly detail 59
Attunements that 'go wrong' 60
Chill out, Dude! 61

Declutter your treatment rituals 63

Time for a Reiki spring clean? 63
Keep at least one hand on the body at all times for fear of losing your connection 64
Treat from head to toe and then you must go back up the body from feet to head 64
Always throw out 'negative' energy at the end of treatment 65
Always 'ground' the energy at the end of a treatment by putting your hands on the floor 65
Recite a set of words at the start of a treatment that 'have' to be said 66
Over to you 67

Reiki treatments and winning the lottery 69

Let's talk about cause and effect 69
Reiki and the lottery 69

4

How do we know whether something was because of the Reiki? 70
So what does Reiki do for people then? 70
The decluttering effect 71
Over to you 71

Reiki is not all fluffy bunnies! 73

When Reiki shifts up a gear 73
Emotional shifts 74
Physical shifts 75
Aftershocks 75
Over to you 75

The Kaizen of Reiki 77

"Kaizen" is in the Reiki precepts 77
Root your practice of Reiki in daily energy work. 78
Receive spiritual empowerments throughout your training and beyond 81
Work on developing your intuitive potential. 82
Learn to become the energies. 82
Live your life according to Usui's guiding principles 83

Get out of the way! 85

"Necessary bystanders" 85
Having a neutral intent 86
Giving treatments while distracted 87

Reiki advice from Bruce Lee: Be like water 89

Excellent advice 89
So how does that echo one's development with Reiki? 90
Emptiness is the goal 91
Over to you 91

Simple energy exercises to get the energy flowing 93

Relax 93
Kenyoku 93
Joshin kokkyu ho 95
Over to you 96

The simplest self-treatment meditation ever! 97

How were you taught to Self-Treat? 97
Taggart's "Meditation with the intention to heal" 97
Over to you 98

Intuitive self-healing meditation 99

Taggart's "Intuitive self-healing meditation" *99*
Over to you *100*

Mikao Usui's original self-treatment meditation.. 101

The Usui self-treatment meditation *101*
Over to you *103*

Intuitive hands-on self-treatment method........... 105

Taggart's Intuitive hands-on self-treatment method *105*
Over to you *106*

The simplest hands-on self-treatment method ever 107

Just rest your hands on yourself and close your eyes *107*
Over to you *107*

The "21 Day" thing.. 109

Where did the 21 day thing come from? *109*
7 x 3 = 21 .... *109*
Don't stop after 21 days! *110*
Over to you *111*

Your 10 day Reiki challenge: the "Releasing Exercise" 113

What is the Releasing Exercise? *113*
How to perform the Releasing Exercise *114*
Stage One *114*
Stage Two *114*
Try this variation *114*
Let Taggart Talk You Through It *115*
Here's what people experienced *115*
Time For You To Take The 10 Day Releasing Exercise Challenge! *119*

Using Reiki for anxiety... 121

Does Reiki work for Anxiety? *121*
What is Anxiety? *121*
How can Reiki help Anxiety? *122*
Reiki energy and Anxiety *122*
Do you already have Reiki? *123*

Using Reiki for stress 125

Can Reiki help with Stress? *125*
Using Reiki for Stress relief *125*
The Reiki precepts and stress *126*

Reiki energy and Stress *127*

Can you send distant healing at Reiki first degree? 129

An unnecessary piece of dogma *129*
Distant Healing at First Degree *130*
Experiment *130*

Restrictions on Reiki 133

The "broken bone" thing *133*
Reiki and pacemakers *134*
Where is the evidence? *135*
Waking up and falling asleep *136*
Cancer, pregnancy, depression, asthma, stress, homoeopathy, animals, medicines *136*
Distant healing *138*

Intelligent Energy? 141

Intuitive working *143*
Hand positions for different ailments *144*

About This Book

This book contains 29 of the 100+ Reiki articles that I have written over the last 20 years. The articles deal with all aspects of practising this beautiful and simple system and I have collected together in this volume the articles best suited to those at Reiki First Degree, the beginner level.

Having said that, though, I think that the articles you will find here should be of interest to and of benefit to all Reiki people at whatever Reiki level.

You will find running through these articles a vision of Reiki as a simple and powerful self-development tool and treatment method, free from the clutter, busyness and dogma of Western Reiki practice.

I root my vision of Reiki in the original practices of Mikao Usui, Reiki's founder, and I try to emphasise the need for simplicity, flexibility, personal dedication and commitment in obtaining the many benefits that are available to the student through Reiki.

How to use this book

Don't read the whole book all in one go. Take your time to work through the essays; there's no rush!

Read an essay or two every day and ponder its contents. Think about your own practice of Reiki and whether what you have read has helped in some way.

For each article, consider:

- Have some of your questions been answered?
- Do you now have further questions?
- Are you prompted to try something new or practise something in a different way?
- Are you prompted to add something to your practice?
- Are you prompted to eliminate something from your practice?

I want you to scribble in this book!

This is a practical workbook, so I want to see you writing in it. Write in it anywhere: underline or circle things, put exclamation marks, arrows and asterisks, jot in the margins, write "NO!!!", write "ABSOLUTELY YES!!", write "NONSENSE!!", write "THIS IS SO TRUE!!".

I hope that these articles make a difference to you and that your practice of Reiki is enhanced as a result.

With best wishes,

Taggart King

Reiki Evolution

www.reiki-evolution.co.uk

Fundamentals

初
傳

Back to Basics: Reiki First Degree

People end up on First Degree courses for many reasons and come from an amazing variety of backgrounds, all attending for their own personal reasons. Reiki courses in the UK present a whole variety of approaches, some "traditional" Western-style, some more Japanese in content, some wildly different and almost unrecognisable, some free and intuitive, others dogmatic and based on rules about what you should always do and not do. Reiki is taught in so many ways, and students will tend to imagine that the way that they were taught is the way that Reiki is taught and practised by most other Reiki people.

What I have tried to do in this article is to present a simple guide to the essence of First Degree: what it's all about and what we should be doing and thinking about to get the most out of our experience of Reiki at this level. My words are addressed to anyone at First Degree level, or anyone who would like to review the essence of First Degree.

First Degree is all about connecting to the energy, learning to develop your sensitivity to the flow of energy, working on yourself to develop your ability as a channel and to enhance self-healing, and working on other people. There are many approaches to doing these things, and I wanted below to touch on each area and to dispel some myths that may have been passed on.

Connecting to the energy

On your Reiki course you will have received some attunements or some empowerments. Attunements are not standard rituals within the world of Reiki and take many forms, some simpler and some more complex. They have evolved and changed greatly during their journey from teacher to teacher in the West. There is no "right way" to carry out an attunement and the individual details of a ritual do not matter a great deal. They all work.

Equally, there is no "correct" number of attunements that have to be carried out at First Degree level. The number four is quoted often as being the "correct" number but this has no basis in Reiki's original form, and whether you receive one, two, three or four rituals on your course, that is fine.

On your course you may have received some "empowerments" rather than attunements, though these are less common. The word "empowerment", or "Reiju empowerment", refers to a connection ritual that has come to us from some Japanese sources, and is closer in essence to the empowerment that Mikao Usui conveyed to his students. Again, there is no correct number of empowerments that has to be carried out. One is enough but it is nice to do more.

What we experience when receiving an attunement or an empowerment will vary a lot. Some people have fireworks and bells and whistles and that's nice for them; other people notice a lot less, very little, or even nothing, and that's fine too. What we feel when we have an attunement is not a guide to how well it has worked for us. Attunements work, and sometimes we will have a strong experience, but it's not compulsory! Whether we have noticed a lot, or very little, the attunement will have given us what we need.

Since in Mikao Usui's system you would have received empowerments from him again and again, it would be nice if you could echo this practice by receiving further empowerments (or attunements) and perhaps these might be available at your teacher's Reiki shares or get-togethers, if they hold them. But it is possible to receive distant Reiju empowerments and various teachers make them freely available as a regular 'broadcast'. This is not essential, and your connection to Reiki once given does not fizzle out, but it would be a beneficial practice if you could receive regular empowerments from someone.

Developing your Sensitivity to the energy

People's experience of energy when they first start working with Reiki can vary. Some people notice more than others, particularly in the early stages, and if we perhaps notice less going on in our hands when compared with another student on the course we can become disillusioned to an extent: that little voice in your head says "I know Reiki works for everyone… but it's not going to work for me. I knew it wasn't going to work for me". Well if this describes your situation then I can say to you that Reiki will work for you, and is working for you, and the vast majority of Reiki people can feel the flow of energy through them in some way, though your particular 'style' of sensing the energy may not involve the more usual heat, fizzing, tingling, pulsing etc. that many people experience.

There are a few Reiki Master/Teachers out there who feel absolutely nothing in their hands, but this is not common, and Reiki is still working for them.

Sensitivity to the flow of energy develops over time, with practice. Some people are lucky enough to be able to feel quite a lot in their hands and in their bodies to begin with, but others have to be patient, trust that Reiki is working for them, and perhaps focus more on the feedback that they receive from the people that they treat, rather than what they feel – or don't feel – in their hands.

It would be worthwhile if all First Degree students spent some time regularly practising feeling energy: between your hands, around your cat or dog or your pot plant or a tree, around someone else's head and shoulders, over someone's supine body, noticing any differences in the sensation in your hands as you move your hands from one place to another.

Don't expect to experience a particular thing or a particular intensity of feeling. Be neutral and simply notice what experience you have and how that experience might change from one area to another.

On some First Degree courses this process will be taught as "scanning", where you hover your hands over the recipient's body, drift your hands from one place to another, and notice any areas which are drawing more energy. This can provide some useful information in terms of suggesting additional or alternative hand-positions to use when you treat, and can suggest areas where you are going to spend longer when you treat.

Working on yourself

It is vital that after going on a First Degree course you establish a regular routine of working on yourself in order to develop your fledgling ability as a channel and to obtain the benefits that Reiki can provide in terms of balancing your life and self-healing. Most people decide to learn Reiki because they are looking for some personal benefits as well as looking to help other people, and the way to get the most out of the Reiki system is to work on yourself regularly.

On your First Degree course you will have been taught a self-treatment method, perhaps a Japanese-style meditation but more likely the Western "hands-on" self-treatment method. You will most likely have been given a set of hand-positions to use, but please remember that these positions are not set in stone and, particularly if some of the hand positions are quite uncomfortable to use in practice, you will develop your own style.

It is fine to change the hand positions based on what feels right from one self-treatment to another, and you should do what feels appropriate. There is no "correct" set of positions that you have to use, and each hand-position does not have to be held for a particular period of time. Treat for however long you have time for, and however long feels right for each hand-position you decide to use.

Many people are taught that they have to do a "21 day self-treat", and some people have the impression that they then do not need to self-treat any more. The "21 day" period has no real basis, and I can say that you ought to be thinking in terms of working on yourself long-term. To gain the greatest benefits from this wonderful system you need to persevere and make working with energy a permanent feature of your life with Reiki, a basic background practice, the effects of which will build up cumulatively as you continue to work with the energy.

You may have been taught a series of energy exercises and meditations called "Hatsurei ho" which comes from Japanese Reiki, and I can commend this practice to you. It is a wonderful way of grounding, balancing, and enhancing you ability as a channel, and should be a regular part of your Reiki routine.

Treating other people

First Degree is also about starting to work on other people, a process which also benefits the giver, so plus points all round really! A few students may have been taught not to treat others at First Degree, or for a particular prescribed period, but this is an unnecessary restriction and Reiki can be shared with other people straight away.

There are many different approaches to treating others, and we should not get bogged down with too many rules and regulations about how we 'must' proceed. Reiki can be approached in quite a regimented way in some lineages, and students may worry that if they are not remembering all the stages that they 'have' to carry out then they will not be carrying out the treatment properly. This is an unnecessary worry because treating other people is simple.

So here is a simple approach that you can use: close your eyes, maybe put your hands in the prayer position, and take a few long deep breaths to calm you and still your mind. You should have in mind that the energy you will channel should be for the highest good of the recipient, but there is no particular form of words that you need to use when commencing your treatment.

Now we are going to focus your attention on connecting to the energy. Imagine that energy is flooding down to you from above, flooding through your crown, through the centre of your body, down to your Dantien (an energy centre two fingerbreadths below your tummy button and 1/3rd of the way into your body). Imagine the energy building up and intensifying there. You are filling with energy.

Now direct your attention towards the recipient and imagine that you are merging with them, becoming one with them. Feel compassion and enjoy the moment.

You may now begin your treatment, and maybe it would be nice to rest your hands on their shoulders for a while, to connect to them and to get the energy flowing. What hand positions you use will vary depending on what you were taught – there are many variations – and they are all variations on a theme, a way of firing the energy from lots of different directions to give it the best chance of getting to where it needs to go.

Hand-positions for treating others are not set in stone and do not have to be followed slavishly.

They are just there as a set of guidelines to follow to build your confidence when treating others, and with time and practice you will start to leave behind these basic instructions and gear any treatment towards the needs of the recipient on that occasion, perhaps based on what you picked up when you were 'scanning' and perhaps based on intuitive impressions, where you feel drawn to a particular area of the body.

Don't try and work out 'why' you have felt drawn to a particular area of the body: just accept your impression and go with it.

Reiki is basically a hands-on treatment method, though for reasons of comfort and propriety you will choose to hover your hands over the recipient in some areas rather than resting on the body. I do not plaster my hands over the recipient's face or throat, for example, because I think that this is uncomfortable and unsettling for the person you are working on.

You do not have to hover your hands for every hand position, as some people are taught, and equally you do not have to keep at least one hand in physical contact with the recipient's body at all times, for fear of 'losing' your connection: your connection to the recipient is a state of mind, and where your hands are is irrelevant!

As you treat, you should aim to feel yourself merging with the energy, becoming one with the energy, to imagine yourself disappearing into the energy, and this can give you a quite blissful experience. Your mind may wander, particularly in the early stages of your Reiki practice, but you do not need to worry about this.

If you notice thoughts intruding, pay them no attention; let them drift on like clouds.

If you make a big effort to try and get rid of your thoughts then you will have in your head the original thoughts and then all the new thoughts about getting rid of the first lot of thoughts… you have made things worse! Just bring your attention gently back to the recipient, to the energy, feel yourself disappearing into the energy, merging with the recipient, and let the energy flow; your treatment can become a wonderful meditation.

It is not acceptable to chat to other people while giving a Reiki treatment.

If you want to be an effective channel for the energy then you need to direct your attention to the work at hand and make sure you are not unduly distracted. For this reason, conversation between yourself and the recipient should be restricted. Reiki works best of you are still and focused, merging with the energy, in a gentle meditative state.

Developing this state takes practice and you can't do it properly if you are chatting.

You do not need to stay for a particular set amount of time for each hand position.

Though it would be probably be best to stay for a few minutes in each position, if in a particular hand position you feel a lot of energy coming through your hands then you can stay in that position for longer – sometimes a lot longer – until the sensation subsides and you can then move onto the next area. Your hands can guide you.

Work from the head and shoulders, down the length of the body, and it is nice to finish with the ankles.

Many people are taught to smooth down the energy field at the end of a session, and that is a nice thing to do, but remember that you do not have to follow any rituals slavishly, particularly in terms of any sort of 'closing' ritual; you do not need to touch the ground, you do not need to say a particular set of words, you do not need to visualise anything in particular, and you do not need to make any 'set' movements of your hands or body.

The Reiki Precepts

On your First Degree course you will have been introduced to the Reiki Precepts, or Reiki Principles, Mikao Usui's "rules to live by'". Just in case you have been given a slightly distorted version of the precepts, here is a more accurate translation:

> *The secret of inviting happiness through many blessings*

The spiritual medicine for all illness

For today only: Do not anger; Do not worry
Be humble
Be honest in your dealings with people
Be compassionate to yourself and others

Do gassho every morning and evening

Keep in your mind and recite

The founder, Usui Mikao

Any reference to 'honouring your elders, parents and teachers' is a later addition to the list, and is not what Mikao Usui taught.

The precepts were the hub of the whole system, and it is said that as much spiritual development can come through following the precepts in your daily life as would come from any energy work, so they are important.

If we can try to focus on living in the moment, not forever dwelling on the past or worrying about the future (fear is a distraction), if we can remind ourselves of the many blessings we have in our lives, if we can forgive ourselves for not being perfect and if we can see things from another's point of view, if we can be compassionate towards ourselves as well as others, then we have gone a long way towards ac hieving a liberating sense of serenity and contentment. This is not something to be achieved overnight, of course: it is a work-in-progress.

Finally

Reiki has the potential to make an amazing, positive difference to you and the people around you. Remember that Reiki is simplicity itself, and by taking some steps to work on yourself regularly, and share Reiki with the people close to you, you are embarking on a very special journey.

How far you travel on that journey is governed by how many steps you take.

The Precepts

Mikao Usui gave his students a series of 'precepts' to follow. The Concise Oxford Dictionary (9th Edition) defines a precept as (1) a command, a rule of conduct, and (2) a moral instruction, and they are an important part of Buddhist practice.

We know that Mikao Usui was a Tendai Buddhist, and so precepts would have been an important part of his spiritual life. Lay followers of Buddhism generally undertake to follow (at least one of) five precepts, which are given in the form of promises to oneself: "I will (try) to...". Here are the five Buddhist precepts:

1. To refrain from harming living creatures (killing).
2. To refrain from taking that which is not freely given (stealing).
3. To refrain from sexual misconduct.
4. To refrain from incorrect speech (lying, harsh language, slander, idle chit-chat).
5. To refrain from intoxicants which lead to loss of mindfulness.

So precepts are a list of guidelines for living your life. They are not framed in terms of "thou shalt not..." as in the Judaeo-Christian tradition but rather are a set of ideals to work towards, recommendations about thought and behaviour that you should follow as much as you can.

Everyone who has learned Reiki will have, or should have, seen the Reiki precepts – Mikao Usui's 'rules to live by' – and they are available in a variety of different forms in different lineages.

Usui's precepts aren't what is commonly taught in the West

There is actually some difference between the precepts that Mikao Usui was teaching and the precepts that are quoted commonly in the West. For example, some Western versions of the precepts include an extra item: "honour your parents, elders and teachers". This is not original and seems to have been added by Mrs Takata to make the "list of rules to live by" more acceptable to her (largely) Christian American audience.

There has been some speculation about where Mikao Usui's precepts come from. It has been claimed that they originate in a book that was published in Usui's time, and it has been claimed that they are based on the edicts of Mutsuhito, the Meiji Emperor.

Certainly it seems that many Tendai and Zen Buddhist teachers were passing on similar principles in Usui Sensei's time.

But now we know that Usui's precepts were his wording of an earlier set of precepts that have been traced back to the early 9th century, precepts that were used in a Tendai sect of Shugendo with which Usui Sensei was in contact.

These precepts were a way of addressing aspects of the Buddhist eight-fold path in a simplified form, and they are the very 'hub' of the whole system.

The precepts were the baseline, the foundation of Usui Sensei's teachings, and it was thought that individual could achieve as much spiritual development by following the precepts as could be achieved by carrying out all the energy exercises.

Aren't negative affirmations a bad idea?

Incidentally, you may find some commentators saying that negative affirmations are not a good idea: such things are said to be more effective when framed in positive terms.

What we have presented to us in the precepts is just a quirk of translation from Japanese to English: the precepts are actually a recommendation that we exist in the moment in a state where we are free from anger and worry, a 'worry-free, anger-free' state.

For me, Mikao Usui's precepts represent both some of the beneficial effects that Reiki can produce in your life if you work with the energy regularly, and they represent a set of principles that we need to follow to enhance our journey of self-healing and self-development with Reiki.

My main purpose in writing this article is to introduce you to a way of working with the precepts in conjunction with the Reiki energy. This is something that I have been experimenting with: a way of directly experiencing the effects of a precept in terms of energy flow.

I would like to suggest that you do the following, for a couple of minutes at a time, twice a day, for a month: Sit with your eyes closed and your hands resting in your lap, palms up. You are going to be releasing energy through your hands.

Stage One

Sit comfortably with your eyes closed and your hands resting in your lap, palms up. Take a few long deep breaths and feel yourself becoming peaceful and relaxed. Your mind empties.

Say to yourself "I now release all my anger..."; say this three times to yourself if you like. Allow energy to be released through your palms, and be still until the flow of energy subsides.

This may take a little while, particularly the first time you try this exercise.

Stage Two

Now say to yourself "I now release all my worry..."; say this three times to yourself if you like.

Again allow a flurry of energy to leave your hands and be still until it subsides. Again this may take a little while, particularly the first time you try this exercise.

Alternatively, try carrying out the releasing exercise in time with your breath.

Breathe in gently, say to yourself "I now release all my anger..." and then breathe out, allowing your anger to flood out of you on the out breath. Gently breath in, and repeat.

Mindfulness and Compassion

In this article I want to talk about Mindfulness and Compassion, which I believe are two essential components of Reiki practice. Whether we are treating others, working on ourselves, empowering others or living our lives with Reiki, we should grow to embody those two states, the essence of the Reiki precepts.

Mindfulness

According to Usui Sensei's surviving students, Mikao Usui introduced his students to the practice of mindfulness at First Degree level, and emphasised this more at Second Degree level. According to the Concise Oxford Dictionary (9th Edition), to be mindful is to take heed or care, to be conscious.

Mindfulness or being mindful is being aware of your present moment. You are not judging, reflecting or thinking. You are simply observing the moment in which you find yourself, fully aware. Moments are like a breath. Each breath is replaced by the next breath. You are there with no other purpose than being awake and aware of that moment.

So mindfulness is a state of living in the moment, of being relaxed, calm and fully engaged in what we are doing. Mindfulness is being fully aware of what is happening right now and giving ourselves completely to our task without distraction. By learning how to enjoy and be in the present moment we can find peace within ourselves.

Like precepts, mindfulness is largely associated with Buddhism and it is a meditative practice that is not reserved for special meditation sessions: it is a practice that you can embrace as part of your daily life and when carrying out routine and mundane tasks.

The best guide that I have found to the use of mindfulness as part of your daily life is the following book, written by Thich Nhat Hanh: "The Miracle of Mindfulness" and I recommend that all Reiki practitioners and teachers obtain a copy and practise being mindful during their daily activities.

I believe that Mikao Usui's precepts are all about mindfulness, and that when we are exhorted by the precepts to "just for today" release anger and worry, we are being guided to exist as far as we can in a mindful state.

Anger and worry are distractions, you see, and if we can exist in the moment by being mindful then we will not dwell on the past and beat ourselves up for things that did not go the way we wanted, and we will not dwell on the future, perhaps worrying about things that have not yet happened.

We can learn to release our attachments to the past and the future and just "be" now, content and accepting in the moment, by learning to be mindful.

Compassion

The final precept, that of being "compassionate towards ourselves and others" is for me an exhortation to be gentle with ourselves, to be patient, to be light-hearted, to not take ourselves quite so seriously and above all to be forgiving – first of all of ourselves but also of others. By accepting and forgiving ourselves we start to release our anger and our worry, and move towards a state of contentment in the moment.

The original system was a spiritual path, a path to enlightenment, and the precepts were what Usui Sensei's system was all about. These principles are a foundation for everything we do with Reiki: the states of mindfulness and compassion arise from following the precepts and from working with Reiki.

For example, how do we feel when we carry out a Reiki treatment? Treating someone with Reiki is a special, special gift. We feel a closeness, an intimacy, a merging with the recipient; we receive trust and we experience compassion. Ideally we should just be there in the moment, with the energy, with the recipient, with no expectations.

We do not treat someone with the intention to resolve their health problem or eliminate their headache. We just merge with the energy and allow Reiki to do its work; we create a sacred space for healing to occur. If our mind wanders, as it may do, then we notice this and gently but firmly bring our attention back to the present and what we are doing. We become one with the energy as it flows through us, we become one with the recipient, and we experience that blissful contentment in the moment.

When we treat we are mindful: we are an observer, not a participant.

Though some are taught that you can hold a conversation with someone as you treat, or watch television at the same time, this really will not lead to the best being given to the recipient. To be the most effective channel we can be, we need to be there with the energy, fully and gently engaged in our work, giving ourselves fully to the task without distraction.

Those same principles apply when working on ourselves, whether carrying out Hatsurei ho or self-treating. The state we should seek to achieve is that of being fully engaged in the endeavour, of being with the energy without distraction, merged, aware and simply existing in the moment, with a gentle feeling of forgiveness, love and compassion towards ourselves.

So both Mindfulness and Compassion are fundamental to our life with Reiki, fundamental to the Reiki precepts, to working on others and working on ourselves.

Not surprisingly they are also an essential component of the transmission of Reiki to another person through carrying out Reiju empowerments. Reiju is the 'connection ritual' that Usui Sensei used, and taught to his surviving students. It is simple, elegant and powerful, free from the clutter and detail that surrounds most Western attunement styles.

When we perform Reiju we have no expectations: we are there in the moment with the energy, following the prescribed movements. We are relaxed and fully engaged in what we are doing, aware of what is happening right now, and we give ourselves completely to our task without distraction. That is the essence of Reiju, the essence of treatments, the essence of the precepts, and the essence of our life with Reiki.

How to start a Reiki treatment

A simple ritual to get your Reiki treatment started

People in different lineages are taught different ways of starting off a Reiki treatment – the ritual(s) that you carry out to get things started – and I thought it would be useful to share with you the sequence that we teach on Reiki Evolution courses, so that you can compare it with what you were taught.

It might trigger off some ideas and help you to develop your own way of doing things if you wanted to.

When standing by the recipient, our students are taught to go through a sequence represented by the letters A, C, B, M, F.

A = Affirm
C = Connect
B = Build
M = Merge
F = Flow

Below I describe these stages in a bit more detail…

Affirm

It's quite common, I think, for Reiki people to make some sort of affirmation or dedication before starting a Reiki treatment, and we have students silently affirm, "I dedicate this treatment to the highest good of [client's name]".

It's just a nice way of reminding yourself that when you carry out a Reiki treatment, you do so in a 'neutral' way, with no expectation of a particular result, metaphorically standing aside to allow the energy to be drawn by the recipient to where it needs to go. So you're setting the right intent.

Once you have gone through this process again and again with different clients, you probably don't need to keep on reminding and re-reminding yourself at the start of each session: you know what your intent is.

Connect

Here is where we focus our attention on our 'connection' to the energy, and we have our students imagine that energy is flowing down through their crown, down through the centre of the body to the Tanden.

And just focusing on that for a little while can bring a lovely meditative state, ideal for carrying out a Reiki treatment on someone.

Build

Now we direct our attention towards the Tanden, that energy centre two finger-breadths below your tummy button and 1/3rd of the way into your body.

This is the centre of your personal universe, the location of your intuition and creativity, a part of the body that is focused on in many traditional practices, for example martial arts, flower arranging, even the tea ceremony.

Here we notice that the energy starts to build here, strengthening and intensifying.

Merge

Having focused on our 'connection' to the energy and the building up of Reiki within us, now we move our attention to the recipient on the treatment table before us, imagining that we are merging with them, becoming one with them, experiencing a state of oneness.

We are neutral, empty, with no expectations, a necessary bystander in the process that is to follow.

Flow

And finally, we allow the energy to flow, drawn by the recipient to the most appropriate places for them on that occasion.

We have established ourselves as a clear channel, a free-flowing conduit, stepping aside metaphorically to allow the energy to be drawn by the recipient, creating a 'healing space' that they can use for their highest good.

We follow the flow of energy, resting our hands in the areas that are drawing the most energy, staying there for as long as the energy needs to flow there, resting our hands in just the right places for that person on that occasion.

Though intuitive working is something that we focus on mainly on our Second Degree courses, some of our First Degree students find that they are already feeling guided by the energy and we encourage them to go with the flow, 'getting out of the way' – not worrying or trying to puzzle out why you are being drawn to a particular area, just letting it happen.

Nice and simple

So there is a simple sequence that you can follow.

I really like the way that it flows from a simple affirmation, noticing your connection to the energy and building the energy within you, moving your attention towards the recipient, merging with them and allowing the energy to flow.

It's like a lovely meditative dance with the energy.

Over to you

If this sequence differs from what you are doing currently, why not try it and see how you get on with it. And post a message below to let me know how it went.

Maybe there is something that you could incorporate into your own ritual, whatever that might be.

None of these things are set in stone, of course, and you can find your own distinctive way, so I hope the above has been helpful to you.

What hand positions should I use?

Are there hand positions that you should always use?

In some Reiki lineages, students are taught 'the' hand positions that they need to use, 'the' twelve hand positions, as if it were set in stone.

But do Reiki treatments really need to follow a set format, no matter what the energy needs of the client? Does every client have to be treated in exactly the same way?

I believe that having a set of hand positions to follow when you are starting out on your Reiki journey is very useful: you have some basic instructions to follow, you don't need to worry, and you can concentrate on getting used to working with the energy, becoming comfortable with being with people in a treatment setting.

You are firing the energy from lots of different directions to make sure it has the best chance to get to where it needs to.

But this 'one size fits all' approach is a bit limiting. Not everyone is the same, so why would we apply the same hand positions to everybody we treat?

So how might we start to adjust or alter where we are resting our hands?

Varying your hand positions for each client

There are two ways to adjust the hand positions that you use: through scanning and through intuition.

Scanning

"Scanning" is taught on most Reiki course and it is a way of finding out where the energy is flowing to on the client's body in the greatest amounts. Energy flowing strongly gives people a variety of sensations, and common feelings might be heat in your hands, or warmth, fizzing, tingling, buzzing, throbbing, heaviness, a magnetic feeling etc.

You hover your hands a few inches away from the client, drift your hand from one place to another, or sweep from one area to another, and focus your attention on the sensations that you are getting on your hand/fingers.

When doing this, you may notice that there are areas of need that don't tie in with the standard hand positions that you are taught, and you could add an extra hand position when you get that part of the body during your treatment, or alter the hand positions away from the standard ones, to accommodate this area of need.

Working intuitively

Intuition is another approach that can be used to gear your treatment more towards the energy needs of the person that you are working on.

Intuition can express itself in a person in different ways: a general 'impression', a feeling of being 'drawn' to an area of the body, an 'inner knowing', or you may find that your hands are drifting apparently of their own accord to some area. This latter approach is something that we teach on our Reiki courses, in the form of "Reiji ho", an intuitive approach that derives from Japanese Reiki.

So after starting off your treatment in whatever way you do that, you could then simply follow your impressions about where to rest your hands, and go with the flow.

How long should I spend in each hand position?

Treat like clockwork?

In some Reiki lineages, students are taught to spend a set amount of time treating each hand position, no matter who they are working on, and some practitioners use audio CDs with little 'bells' that sound out every three minutes, say.

But isn't this a bit mechanical, and everyone's different, so why would we give essentially the same treatment to everyone that we work on?

Altering your treatments to suit the client

The energy needs of each person that we work on will be different, so it's reasonable to expect each Reiki treatment that we give to be different, based on the individual energy needs of the client.

I don't think we should treat everyone like a "Reiki robot", changing hand position every time a bell pings, no matter what the client's energy system needs on that occasion. In my article "What hand positions should I use?" I spoke about moving beyond the standard hand positions that are taught in some lineages, and we can also move beyond the idea of treating for the same amount of time in each hand position.

Clients will have areas of the body that need Reiki more than others, so it makes sense to spend longer in these areas of need, and to spend less time in areas where there's not such a great need for Reiki to flow.

How to know how long to take in one position

So how can we work out how long we should spend in each hand position? I would like to suggest two methods, one based on sensing the flow of energy, and one based on intuition.

Most Reiki people can feel the flow of energy through their hands, which often shows itself as heat, fizzing, tingling, buzzing, heaviness, a magnetic feeling or whatever, if you can feel the flow of energy through your hands then you will be able to tell whether the hand position you are using is drawing lots of energy.

Sometimes it's completely clear, since your hands are absolutely 'on fire'!

It would be a good idea to stay in that hand position for longer, and after a while you will start to notice that the flow of energy – and associates sensations – starts to reduce in intensity.

When things have calmed down, move onto your next hand position.

We can also allow our intuition to guide us in terms of how long we spend working on a particular part of the body. Everyone is intuitive, and our intuition can make itself known to us in different ways. We may feel 'locked' into a particular hand position, or have an 'inner knowing' that we should stay where we are for the time being.

One little trick that I have used in the past to tell whether I need to stay where I am or move on involves using a visualisation that connects to your inner knowing: when treating someone, and I'm wondering whether I should move on now, I have an imaginary hand appear in my mind's eye, resting where my real hand is.

I imagine that this imaginary hand moves away from the body, as if on a piece of elastic, and if the imaginary hand wants to pull itself back to its original position, pulled by the elastic, then I should stay there for longer.

If the hand seems happy to drift away, in my mind's eye, then I know it's ok to move on to a new position… just a little visualisation that you can use to access intuitive knowledge.

Over to you

If these approaches are new to you, why not try them and see what happens, and let us know about your experiences by posting a message below.

Or maybe you started out doing treatments with standard timings, and now you don't.

How did that happen, and what do you think about the quality of your treatments now that you're working more freestyle?

Do I need to keep at least one hand on a person when I treat them?

Keep touching or you'll lose the 'connection'?

In some lineages, students are taught that they always need to keep at least one hand resting on the body at all times because, if they do not, they will 'lose their connection' with the client, and then have to go through a ritual again in order to regain that lost connection.

But is this really necessary?

Do we have to have to touch the body every second, like a sort of Reiki tag-team, for fear of disconnecting, and is the Reiki 'connection' so fragile?

What's the difference between hands-on and hands-off?

I believe that there is no difference between a Reiki treatment carried out when hands are resting on the body, and treatments where hands hover over the body.

Reiki is generally carried out as a 'hands-on' therapy and I think that this is a good idea: there is something very special and healing about human touch, with or without the addition of Reiki, and that closeness or connection that comes through making physical contact with another person is an important part of the Reiki experience.

Of course there are times – and hand positions – where it is better for the sake of propriety and respect to keep your hands off the body, particularly when working intuitively, when hands can end up wanting to go goodness-knows-where, and it's not always wise to always put your hands down where they want to come to rest!

Basically Reiki is a hands-on practice

Viewing Reiki as a hands-on practice, though, does not mean that we have to keep our hands on the body at all times. We can mix-and-match, resting on the body sometimes and hovering over the body at other times during the course of a treatment, and we can do both at the same time: resting one hand on the body while allowing the other hand to hover.

If we are always keeping a hand on the body for fear of losing our 'connection', I wonder what we think that connection is all about.

Distant healing is a standard part of Reiki practice, where you can send the energy to the other side of the planet if we like, just by focusing our attention on the recipient. If we can do that then why would we believe that, at the same time, we can't send Reiki to a person on a treatment couch in front of us – just inches away from us – unless we've made physical contact with them?

It makes no sense at all. 1,000 miles away and sending Reiki's no problem… six inches away and we lose our connection if we're not touching the body. How can that be?

How are we connected?

So what is our Reiki 'connection' to the recipient?

I believe our 'connection' to them is based on our state of mind: by focusing our attention on the recipient we connect to them.

If we think about the Buddhist origins of Reiki and the concept of oneness, there is no 'us' and there is no 'them' anyway: this is illusion! We are already 'connected' to them because in reality we were never separated from them.

We are them.

So, in practice, by being with a client in the same room for the purposes of giving and receiving Reiki, we merge with them, we begin to become one with them. It is our intention that underlies our connection and the energy flows to where our attention is directed, whether our hands are on the body or not.

Over to you

Were you taught that you need to have at least one hand on your client at all times for fear of losing your connection? If so, what has happened in practice? Have you experimented with both-hands-on, one-hand-on and no-hands on?

What feedback have you received from clients where you didn't follow the rules that you were given?

And what do you think about your 'connection' to your client? Do you think it depends on physical contact with them?

Reiki Sensations

In this article I would like to talk about the sort of things that students might feel – or not feel – when receiving attunements or empowerments, when working with energy and when treating or being treated, and the significance of these sensations.

The article is particular addressed to people who have just taken a First Degree course or who are only just starting on their journey with Reiki, though it should be of interest to people at all Reiki levels.

Attunements or empowerments

(Please note that, to avoid unnecessary repetition, I am going to use the word 'empowerment' to refer both to Reiju empowerments and Western-style Reiki attunements.)

When we arrive on a Reiki First Degree course, we probably have very little idea of what we might experience when going through an empowerment. If you read books about Reiki, everyone seems to be going through an exceptional, once-in-a-lifetime experience, but for most people it really isn't like that.

There is no way of predicting what an individual will experience when receiving an empowerment, whether in person or at a distance. You may have an amazing experience, or you may feel very little or nothing. It is not uncommon for people to see some colours or feel some heat or tingling or pulsing or pressure in various areas of their bodies. For some people an empowerment is a unique experience, profound, emotional, an experience that is almost unbelievable. For others very little happens.

Sometimes you might find that there will be four people, say, on a course. Three people are talking about the surprising, or interesting, or special experiences that they just had, and one poor soul is sitting there thinking to themselves "I knew this wouldn't work for me... I know Reiki is supposed to work for everyone, but it hasn't worked for me".

We assume that if we notice a lot happening then the empowerment has 'taken', that it has worked really well, and we assume that if we felt very little – or if we felt nothing – then the connection ritual has not worked, that we haven't been attuned, or we haven't been attuned properly.

But what a student experiences when they receive an empowerment is no guide as to the effectiveness of that empowerment. In fact what a student experiences really is irrelevant, because empowerments always work.

Of course it is nice and reassuring to have the "bells and whistles and fireworks" – it helps you to believe that something definite has happened - but someone who has noticed all these things has not been more effectively empowered when compared with a student who felt very little or nothing.

Experiences are interesting, but not important. They don't mean anything in terms of whether, or how well, an empowerment has worked, because empowerments always work, no matter what the student feels or doesn't feel.

Experiencing energy

People are all different, and people differ in terms of how sensitive they are to the flow of energy in the early stages of their work with Reiki. Sometimes people arrive on a Reiki course massively sensitive to the energy, and perhaps better able to sense subtle differences than is their teacher, and that's nice for them, while other people may notice something very subtle, or perhaps nothing at all. Most people will feel something.

So when playing with energy, most people will feel something in between their hands when they try to make an energy ball. Most people will feel something when they try to feel someone else's energy field, or if they practise 'scanning' (assuming that there is something there to detect – there won't always be). But not everyone will feel these things to begin with, and the people who do not feel anything should not be disheartened: because sensitivity to such things can develop with practice and repetition.

Most people will find that, no matter how sensitive they find themselves when they first learn Reiki, when they start to work with the energy regularly – for example by carrying out Hatsurei ho every day, and by self-treating – their sensitivity to the energy will increase. But this is a work-in-progress and we may need to be patient. And we may find that our sensitivity to the energy never reaches our goal, or is never as great as other Reiki people that we come across. Maybe we are setting an unreasonable target for ourselves.

And we should remember that sensitivity to the flow of energy is not the be-all and end-all of Reiki. We can work on ourselves and derive the many benefits that come through Reiki, no matter what we feel or don't feel when we carry out hatsurei ho or self-treat. We can treat other people effectively no matter what we might feel or not feel in our hands.

I have come across several successful and effective Reiki Master / Teachers who do not feel anything going on in their hands, and never have done. The reason why they continued their Reiki training, rather than giving up in the face of no physical sensations to encourage them, was because they practised on lots of people and they could see, by the positive responses they received from the recipients, that something was definitely going on, that they were doing good things, that Reiki was certainly doing something for the people they treated even though they couldn't feel the energy.

You may ask how you can treat someone when you can't feel anything, or if you can't scan very well at the moment. Well, most people in the world of Reiki are taught a standard set of hand positions to use when they treat, and these standard positions can be followed, giving general coverage over the body; the energy is drawn to areas of need, so that works perfectly well. Not everyone scans.

Not everyone is taught how to scan. It isn't a vital step in a treatment, but it can be a useful one to perform if you can do it.

But if you can work intuitively then of course you can place your hands in the right places for each person you work on, and stay in each position for the most appropriate amount of time, not based on the sensations you are feeling in your hands but based on your intuitive impressions.

Everyone can work intuitively with some practice, and you may well be taught how to carry out "Reiji ho" (a Japanese method for opening to your intuition during a treatment) on a Second Degree course. So an intuitive approach to treatments actually eliminates any advantage in being able to sense strongly in your hands.

Sensations experienced by people you treat

Now, you will not be surprised to know that the experiences of people being treated also varies a great deal. For some people, on some occasions, treatments are very strong. They might feel intense heat from the practitioner's hands, see coloured lights, drift in and out of consciousness. And on other occasions that same person might feel the treatment to be mild and gentle.

The energy is drawn by the recipient in amounts that are appropriate for them on that occasion, so the perceived 'strength' of any treatment is determined by the recipient's need. The practitioner is just a necessary bystander in the treatment process.

While some people seem to quite often notice a lot happening when they are treated, there are also people who feel very little or nothing when they receive a Reiki treatment, no matter who they receive the treatment from.

If you have just started out on your Reiki journey and you just happen to treat one of these people, or a few of these people, as your first 'clients' then you may end up disheartened, thinking that their lack of a strong sensation means that you are ineffective as a practitioner.

We want the recipient to feel a lot because that reassures us that we are doing things 'correctly', that we are effective as a channel for the energy. But things aren't always so simple: while quite often there may be general correlation between what the practitioner feels and what the recipient feels (a very hot area for the practitioner is felt as a very tingly area, say, for the recipient) this correlation will not always be there and, sometimes, you might find a practitioner feeling a raging furnace in their hands, amazed at the strength of what is going on, while the recipient did not notice anything at all, and perhaps didn't notice anything at all during the entire treatment!

Summary

So really this whole article boils down to one simple phrase: "just for today, do not worry". While it is perfectly natural to want to have some physical sensations to help us believe that we are really doing something when we use

Reiki on ourselves and on other people, and while most people who learn Reiki will receive sufficient feedback to reassure them, this will not always happen.

With practice and experience we start to let go of the need to be reassured by what we and others feel, and we come to realise that no matter what we feel or don't feel, Reiki is working for us. But it can be difficult to accept this in the early stages, particularly if we are a little sceptical.

If you aren't feeling too much at the moment my advice to you is to follow the instructions you were given: carry out your Hatsurei ho every day, self-treat regularly, and get your hands on as many people as you can.

Do short blasts on someone's knee or shoulder, treat people in a straight-backed chair for 20-30 minutes, do full treatments; go with the time you have you have available.

The important thing is to get the hands-on practice and you will find, if you treat a good cross-section of people, that you will receive from them the positive feedback that you need, and with sufficient practice you may find that you start to notice more with time.

So be patient, don't worry, and have fun with your Reiki.

Treating both sides: is this necessary?

An unnecessary Reiki rule?

In many Reiki lineages, students are taught that they need to treat both sides of a client, asking them to turn over half-way through a treatment so that student can gain access to the client's back. But is this really necessary?

Might the treatment be just as effective if we left them where they were?

I think that most Reiki people would accept that when we treat someone, the energy is drawn according to the recipient's need to the right places for them on that occasion, to do whatever they need to have done on that occasion, so we aren't 'pushing' the energy to where we want it to (or think it ought to) go.

We are a necessary bystander in the process: we need to be there for the healing to happen, but we have metaphorically stepped aside, created a 'healing space' for the client, and they do the healing that they need to do, in the way that they need to do it, experiencing whatever is appropriate for them to experience as this happens.

Could we just hold their hand for 60 minutes?

So, in theory, we could just hold someone's hand for an hour and the energy would be drawn by them to the areas of need, and we'd need to do nothing further than that.

But given that when we work intuitively we can be drawn strongly to areas of need – 'hotspots' – and given that we can experience the flow of energy subsiding in those areas after a time, and given that when we work intuitively we can be guided to hold a series of hand positions, sometimes symmetrical, sometimes not, in a particular sequence, this suggests to me that there is value in allowing the energy to guide you (which is what I believe is happening when you work intuitively), and there is a value in placing your hands in different positions as you treat.

There is something special, I believe, in working in partnership with the energy and allowing it to guide you in terms of where you rest your hands, and for how long you hold each position.

So going through a series of hand positions, whether a set of 'standard' positions or intuitively-guided hand positions, helps to 'fire' the energy from lots of different directions, and it's drawn into the areas that have the greatest need.

We don't just treat the square inches underneath our palms

The energy doesn't just go into a small area of the body underneath our hands when we treat: it moves through the body and you could imagine the energy travelling to chakras, through meridians, into the aura, into all the different aspects of the energy system, physical, mental, emotional, spiritual, whether or not we 'sent' the energy there, because it's being pulled by the recipient's need.

Many of us will have experienced the situation where you're treating one part of the body and the client comments that they can feel the heat, or coldness, or tingling or whatever in a different part of their body.

And because the energy will move from where we 'put it' to where it is needed, this suggests that we do not need to place our hands on every square inch of the body in order for a treatment to be successful, and I do not believe that it is necessary to specifically 'treat' the back in order for the energy to flow to the back of the body from wherever we place our hands.

Turning over routinely is so disruptive

On a practical note, disrupting the flow of a treatment so that the client has to wake up half way through, drag themselves half into the seated position and turn themselves over and get comfortable again, really does break the 'spell' that they are under and, since the relaxation that people experience when receiving Reiki is greatly beneficial, I wouldn't want to wake them up and lessen the depth of their relaxation in this way routinely.

That's not to say that I never treat people's backs, of course.

No rules should be followed slavishly.

But I only do this when someone has a specific back problem and what I do is to start by treating the back for a while, and then turn them over into the 'face-up' treatment position, and carry on with majority of their treatment that way.

In fact, in my First Degree manual I provide a series of hand positions that you can use when treating backs. But I don't recommend that you do that routinely because it's not necessary.

Over to you

If you routinely turn people over half way through a treatment, why not try not doing this and see what happens?

What if I get it wrong?

Getting anxious about our Reiki

When we go on a Reiki course, whether at First Degree, Second Degree or Master Teacher level, we are given instructions telling us how to carry out various tasks, and if we are conscientious then we will try our best to follow those instructions to make sure that we are 'doing it properly'.

So whether we are treating ourselves, giving someone else a Reiki treatment, or performing an attunement on a student, we hope to achieve the desired results by doing it right, by following the instructions to the letter, and if it appears to us that the desired results have not been achieved then we tend to surmise that we have not followed the instructions properly, that we have forgotten something vital and done it wrong, and we may believe that the lack of an expected result is our fault.

If only we could have done things properly then things would have been different.

But there are two problems with this.

Firstly, in reality, not following all the instructions will have very little effect on the efficacy of our treatment or attunement and, secondly, a lack of an expected response or result does not mean that we have done it wrong, or that something has not worked properly.

Treatments that 'go wrong'

Let's think about Reiki treatments for a while.

We have been given a set procedure to follow by our teacher and perhaps we have a certain ritual to carry out before we commence the hands-on treatment. Perhaps we have been given a standard set of hand positions to follow or a set of things that we are 'supposed' to do at the end of a treatment, to bring things to a close.

We carry out the treatment and then the recipient says that they didn't feel very much, or they didn't feel anything at all, or they felt unsettled and not relaxed, and we think back and realise that we missed one of the 'introductory' stages, or we got the words wrong, or we forgot to say something, or we used the 'wrong' sequence of hand positions, or we missed out a hand position or two, or neglected to carry out one of the closing stages of the treatment.

Because the treatment 'didn't work' (apparently) we then assume that this is because we got the treatment wrong, we did the wrong thing, we forgot a vital stage, and it's all our fault.

But we should remind ourselves that not everyone in the world of Reiki is taught to carry out treatments in exactly the same way. Other people may have stages to go through and phrases to say that are very different from how you were taught; they may not have even heard of half the things that you were taught to do, and yet their treatments work perfectly well.

Should we assume that they are not doing things properly because they are not doing it the same way as you?

Or should we assume that your treatment is inadequate because you are missing out vital stages that other people were taught to go through?

Of course not: there are many different ways of approaching giving Reiki treatments, different traditions, different styles, different flavours, some simple, some complex, and they all achieve the desired results.

So we should realise that the 'vital' stages that we were taught to go through are perhaps not quite so vital as we first thought. Reiki accommodates many different ways of working and no phrase or hand movement or ritual is absolutely necessary.

Reiki is above all that fiddly detail

It doesn't matter.

What matters when you treat someone is that you focus your attention on the person you are working on, that you feel yourself merging with the energy and the person in front of you, that you allow yourself to disappear into the energy, neutral, empty, no expectations, and just let it happen.

Anything else beyond that is just frippery, icing on a cake that was fine when it was plain.

We don't need to gild the lily, we don't need to adorn unnecessarily something that was already beautiful, or to make superfluous additions to what is already complete.

So follow the instructions that you were given, by all means, but don't fret if you don't follow the sequence exactly, and please allow yourself the freedom to tailor your routine according to what feels right for you; find your own style and comfortable way of working rather than slavishly following a set of instructions passed on to you by another person.

Go with what feels right for you on that occasion; be guided by intuition.

And why should we assume that the treatment did not work, that the session did not give the recipient what they needed, just because they felt very little, or felt nothing happening, or felt unrelaxed during the treatment? While many people have a wonderful time while being treated, seeing coloured lights, feeling tingling sensations or intense heat from the practitioner's hands, experiencing deep relaxation and peace, melting into the treatment table, not everyone experiences that.

Not everyone is the same.

Not all recipients have a great time when they receive Reiki. Some people feel nothing, some feel very little, and some are quite unsettled by the whole experience. But no matter what they noticed happening, they received what they needed, and they experienced whatever sensations they needed to experience.

It's nice to have positive feedback at the end of a treatment session, and people saying how relaxed they were and how hot our hands were etc. helps to boost our confidence, but such things are not compulsory and not everyone will say these things. We didn't mess up their treatment because it would be very difficult to mess up a Reiki treatment: Reiki is foolproof!

Attunements that 'go wrong'

The same comments apply to the carrying out of attunements.

There are very many different attunement styles being used in the world, some quite simple, some quite complicated, and there will be stages and ritual movements or phrases/affirmations being used by some teachers that are not being used all by other teachers.

One teacher may be going through – to them – a vital stage that others do not replicate, while others will be doing 'necessary' practices that we do not follow. And yet all these attunement styles work.

So while we should always try and do our best, and follow the attunement instructions that we were given, we should not worry terribly if we realise that we have missed out a particular stage or forgot to say a particular phrase, or failed to draw a symbol perfectly.

What is important when attuning someone is your underlying intent; the details of the ritual are there to create a ritual 'space' in which the attunement can occur, but there are no really vital stages that have to be carried out no matter what, so we should not worry.

And we should remember that the reaction of a student to an attunement will vary greatly.

If a student feels very little or nothing we should not assume that the attunement has not 'taken'; this would not be possible. Equally, we should not assume that a student who experienced 'bells and whistles' has been far more effectively attuned. Such sensations and experiences are nice for the recipient but do not really indicate anything significant.

Attunements work, even with some mistakes, and sometimes the recipient has an amazing experience; sometimes not.

It doesn't matter what they feel or don't feel.

Chill out, Dude!

So we should feel confident that Reiki is giving the recipient what they need, whether they are receiving a treatment or an attunement, we should try our best and be conscientious but we should not worry too much if we don't follow all the instructions.

We should allow ourselves to find our own style, own comfortable way of working, which may be a little different from other people's but which is just as valid, and we should not assume that a lack of 'bells and whistles' on the part of the recipient means that something hasn't happened.

There is no one 'correct' way to do things, there is no correct response to treatments or attunements, and Reiki accommodates many different styles and approaches.

So we can relax!

Declutter your treatment rituals

Time for a Reiki spring clean?

Reiki treatments are carried out in a lot of different ways and many rituals have been developed and passed on in different lineages.

Reiki has also been affected by the belief systems of people who are involved in other energy practices and it's natural for Reiki teachings to become 'coloured' by a teacher's personal quirks and idiosyncrasies too.

Trouble is, these practices end up turning into "this is the way that you have to do it" as they are passed on from teacher to student, teacher to new teacher, and that's unfortunate since some people end up lumbered with quite complex rituals that they feel they have to carry out for a treatment to be done 'properly'.

Reiki is greater than that.

Reiki works simply and intuitively and doesn't need to be accompanied by a lot of dogma. There will be Reiki practitioners out there who treat their clients using a lot of rituals that other effective Reiki practitioners do not use, and there will be people out there using Reiki effectively while not carrying out stages and rituals that other practitioners regard as essential.

Let's look at a few examples of ideas and practices that I regard as unnecessary.

If you were taught to do these things, why not experiment and find your own approach.

Keep at least one hand on the body at all times for fear of losing your connection

I have written about this one before, and if we can send Reiki from one side of the planet to the other just by thinking of someone, there will be no problem in 'losing' your connection to a client on a treatment table in front of you should your hands stray a few inches from their body.

'Connection' is a state of mind and comes through focusing your attention on the recipient. If you're doing a Reiki treatment on someone then you are connected to them!

Treat from head to toe and then you must go back up the body from feet to head

Seems a bit clumsy to me, and is sometimes combined with the previous paragraph, so you end up with "always keep at least one hand on the body at all times and work from head to foot, and then back to the head again".

The general approach within Reiki seems to be to work from head to feet, though working the other way might be the right thing to do sometimes.

My approach is to work intuitively so I don't follow a set of rules that have to be applied to every client in the same way. Why should every client receive the same format of treatment? They have different problems, different energy needs.

'One size fits all' doesn't fit very well with me.

Always throw out 'negative' energy at the end of treatment

If you believe that there is negative energy and if you believe that it will stay with the client (and presumably cause them problems) if you don't throw it away, then I suppose you'd better throw it away.

And if you've got it on you before you throw it away then presumably you don't want that stuff hanging around on you either, so you really need to throw it away.

But not everyone is taught that and not everyone does that, and some people believe that Reiki is a pure healing energy that is drawn by the recipient's need, and gives the recipient what they need on that occasion, balancing and transforming in a way that is right for them.

And in that case, we wouldn't need to think in terms of accumulating stuff that Reiki couldn't get rid of, and dealing with it ourselves.

Always 'ground' the energy at the end of a treatment by putting your hands on the floor

Some people do seem to have quite a bee in their bonnet on the issue of grounding.

They put almost every malady down to not being grounded, and have their students frantically grounding themselves.

On a personal level, grounding is easy: go for a walk, do the washing up, breathe in some fresh air and you're grounded. Hatsurei ho – daily energy exercises – grounds you.

I believe that giving a Reiki treatment is a grounding exercise.

So what is this ungrounded energy that you have to deal with when you put your hands on the floor – is it your energy, is it the client's "ungrounded" energy, and what would happen if you didn't crouch down and touch the floorboards?

Isn't Reiki a bit more effective than that?

Does it really need us to come along and sort out stuff that it hasn't dealt with properly?

Recite a set of words at the start of a treatment that 'have' to be said

Many people have a set form of words that they say to themselves to get them in the right frame of mind for carrying out a Reiki treatment, and I have no problem with that.

This can be useful and helpful.

But some people are taught that "these words are THE words" that you have to say at the start of the treatment, with the corollary that if you haven't said them, or if you mess up the words, then the treatment's not going to go properly.

If you've said a set of words time and again before starting a treatment, don't you think your subconscious mind knows what it's all about, and that you have that intention 'programmed' into you already?

Intention is a very important thing with Reiki and I don't think you need to keep on reminding and re-reminding yourself about what you want to happen.

Over to you

I hope the above comments have provided some food for thought and if you are currently using the practices described above, why not try a different approach, see what happens, and come to your own conclusions about what's the best way for you to approach treating others.

Have you altered your own approach compared to what you were originally taught, and have you found that leaving behind some of those rules and restrictions has been fine?

Reiki treatments and winning the lottery

Let's talk about cause and effect

Sometimes I am asked by my students about things that happen to a client after they have had a Reiki treatment. The questions are usually framed in terms of:

"After the treatment, this happened… is that the Reiki?"

"I gave someone a treatment and the next week x happened… was that the Reiki?"

Sometimes my response is [shrugs shoulders]… maybe, or "who knows"… sometimes I will say "probably" or "could be".

And that's about as far as I can go because (1) I don't have a crystal ball and (2) not everything that happens to a person after they have had a Reiki treatment, or been on a Reiki course, is a result of the Reiki that they received or were initiated into.

Reiki and the lottery

So someone goes on a Reiki course and the next week they win the lottery. Is Reiki responsible for this? Has the universe conspired in such a way as to bring that person their winning numbers because they decided to learn Reiki?

Someone has a Reiki treatment and the next week they get run over by a 'bus. Is the Reiki responsible for this event?

The answer is no: not everything that happens to a person after Reiki is because of the Reiki.

Because things occur randomly: unusual things happen to people sometimes, things appear out of the blue.

And because we seek to fnd an explanation for the things that happen to us in our lives, we try and attach that happening to something, something different or new that we have done or experienced.

How do we know whether something was because of the Reiki?

You don't.

Not in an individual case.

You can only look at a group of people and see what sort of things they tend to experience after receiving or learning Reiki, and you can find themes emerging, experiences or happenings that seem to turn up again and again and again.

And then when that happens to another student, you can say, "yes, that probably was the Reiki", but you'll never know absolutely definitely because the thing they are reporting may have just happened anyway.

So what does Reiki do for people then?

Whether you receive a course of treatments or if you are learning Reiki for yourself, you should find that Reiki helps you to feel more 'laid back' – calm, content and serene – and you should find that you feel better able to deal with stressful situations or stressful people, and that you feel more positive and better able to cope.

If energy levels are low then they can be boosted; if spirits are low then they can be lifted.

This 'Reiki effect' seems to be noticed in most people who learn Reiki and work on themselves regularly, or in people who receive a course of Reiki treatments.

The decluttering effect

One of the things that I have noticed, based on my experiences when teaching students through my Reiki Home Study courses, is the "decluttering" effect that Reiki can have on many people.

Reiki seems to cause people to want, or to find, a simpler way through their life, and that can involve ditching things: ditching household clutter, ditching unwanted commitments and habits, clearing out cupboards and spare rooms, simplifying your life on lots of levels.

Over to you

So, what things have you experienced as a result of receiving Reiki treatments that you are fairly certain are because of the Reiki?

What changes occurred in your life after you learned Reiki that you're fairly sure are because of the system that you learned?

How has Reiki changed things for the better for you?

Reiki is not all fluffy bunnies!

When Reiki shifts up a gear

We know what Reiki tends to do for people, don't we? People end up chilled, calm, serene, content, better able to cope, more positive.

Reiki brings balance, perspective, and if you add in a regular focus on the Reiki precepts, and the practise of mindfulness, then you have a really powerful system for positive change.

But it's not all happy bunnies and smiles: Reiki can produce powerful effects and elicit powerful shifts in a person.

When someone comes for a Reiki treatment, they will usually have a wonderful experience. They will feel more relaxed than they have for a very long time, they will drift, or float, or sink, they will bliss out on those boiling hot hands, they might have rainbow light shows, or tingles, a lovely experience.

But it's not like that for everyone.

Sometimes a person can just feel generally 'unsettled' during a treatment. They don't relax, they don't necessarily experience anything powerful, but they're not calm and relaxed and peaceful, as most people are. So what is going on here?

Well, they are having a definite experience, the energy is doing something for them, and what it is doing is coming through as that sense of being unsettled.

The energy will provide the recipient with a variety of sensations or feelings, and they are just what that person needs to experience to best shift what they need to shift to move on, a side-effect, in a way, of the energetic work that is going on within them.

Often it's a lovely experience, but not always.

Emotional shifts

Sometimes Reiki can produce powerful emotional effects in a short space of time, as people release what they need to release to move on with their lives.

It's as if all this deeply-embedded stuff is bubbling to the surface to be released.

So I have had people literally wailing on the treatment table, and it's not uncommon to see a silent tear or two pass from someone's eye as they're treated.

And although it's not nice to see someone in distress, it seems that these emotions, although powerful at times, are experienced in a positive way by the client, where there is a sense of relief that they are just letting go, moving on from what they are experiencing on the treatment table.

So don't worry if someone becomes emotional when you treat them. This is common. It shows that things are moving, shifting, and that's what you and your client want.

By the end of the session, everything will have calmed down and your client will feel much better. The treatment will have come like a breath fo fresh air, like a cleansing breath that has flushed out accumulated gunk.

And while your client may sometimes feel a bit shell-shocked by what they experienced, they will have left stuff behind and moved on in some positive fashion.

Physical shifts

While the 'emotional release' is probably more common than its physical counterpart, sometimes a client will experience more physical sensations, for example pain. It's not uncommon for someone with arthritis, for example, to experience a short-term intensification of those joint pains, while they are receiving their treatment, though the pains then subside and often improve subsequently.

I have treated people with metal plates inserted into their bones, where the area has ached during a treatment, for example.

Aftershocks

A Reiki treatment is rather like dropping a pebble into a pond: while there is the initial splash, during the treatment – an intensification of things – the energy will also produce ripples that carry on, with peaks and troughs.

So it's not uncommon for a client to experience some emotional ups and downs in the days after a treatment, with physical effects like better sleep, or disturbed sleep, aches and pains, feeling full of energy, or feeling tired and wanting to change gear and slow down for a while.

These things are all side-effects of the energy working to bring things into balance for that person, giving them the opportunity to re-balance, to reinterpret, to reconsider, to achieve a new state of wellness.

Over to you

What powerful effects have you or witnessed when giving a Reiki treatment? What did your client experience and how did that help them to improve things subsequently?

What have you experienced for yourself when receiving a Reiki treatment that would consider to be a powerful experience, and how has that helped you?

The Kaizen of Reiki

If you have come across the word 'kaizen' before it will probably have been in the context of industrial quality control or personal development.

"Kaizen" is a Japanese word that is usually translated as 'improvement', but it means more than that. The word has connotations of continuous, gradual, orderly and never-ending improvement, the willingness to constantly, relentlessly pursue improvement a small step at a time.

The application of the kaizen principle is the reason why Japan's economy was transformed after the Second World War. All workers were encouraged to make suggestions as to how quality and production could be improved, even by tiny, tiny percentages, but over time the effect of these tiny percentage improvements, applied consistently and built upon, transformed Japanese industry.

So what has this to do with Reiki?

"Kaizen" is in the Reiki precepts

Well the word kaizen actually appears towards the end of the Reiki precepts. The line in Japanese is "Shin shin kaizen, Usui Reiki Ryoho", which could be loosely translated as "Mind body change it for better Usui Reiki method".

So when Usui was talking about using his system to improve the body and mind, I get the impression that we are looking at a lifelong commitment to work with the system, to focus the energy on ourselves again and again, long-term, in order to produce small incremental improvements within ourselves, to dedicate ourselves to developing our effectiveness as a channel.

But small changes build on previous small changes, an enhancement upon an enhancement leads to amazing development over time. And Usui's original system gives us the solid, concrete techniques that we can use to develop ourselves: as channels, in terms of spirituality and in terms of intuition, to produce our own individual Reiki Evolution!

So how do we pursue our own kaizen of Reiki? How do we apply the concept of continuous and never-ending improvement to our practice of Reiki? Here are a few suggestions…

Root your practice of Reiki in daily energy work.

If you are serious about wanting to obtain the many benefits that are available to you through the Reiki system then you are going to have to work on yourself most days, ideally every day, and by doing so you will build up the beneficial effects of Reiki within you.

It is not sufficient to use Reiki on yourself once a week, or to assume that if you treat other people occasionally then this is enough to give you the Reiki you need.

Your first priority should be yourself, and this means daily energy work.

This does not need to be an onerous task, nor does it need to take a long time to carry out. Sometimes we decline to use Reiki on ourselves because we do not have the perfect opportunity, perhaps because we do not have, say, 30 minutes to work on ourselves.

Yet even 10 minutes of energy work, when carried out consistently each day, would be far better and produce much better results than doing nothing for days, and then a great big blitz for a big chunk of time on a weekend to try and 'catch up'.

Spending even a small chunk of time working on ourselves each day builds up a momentum and stirs changes which build and build.

Sporadic practice leads to some beneficial changes, but you are not maximising your Reiki potential.

So, how can we work on ourselves?

Well, a good place to start would be to practise Hatsurei ho, a series of energy exercises taught in the Usui Reiki Ryoho Gakkai (the 'Gakkai), an association set up after Usui's death by the Imperial Officers who had trained with him for a while.

'Hatsurei ho' means something like 'start up Reiki technique' and consists of a series of energy meditations/ visualisations that focus on your Tanden (Dantien in Chinese) and which are designed to be carried out every day.

The effects of Hatsurei ho are to:

1. Clear and cleanse your energy system
2. Help to move your energy system more into a state of balance

3. Help to ground you
4. Help to build up your personal energy reserves
5. Allows you to grow spiritually
6. Develop your ability as a channel for Reiki
7. Help to develop your sensitivity to the flow of energy
8. Help to develop your intuitive side

The exercises take perhaps 12-15 minutes to carry out each day, and can be fitted into the busiest of schedules if the will is there. We can all make this time for our Reiki practice.

But we should also focus the energy more specifically on ourselves, on our own self-healing, by carrying out a self-treatment each day.

Whether you carry out the Western 'hands-on' method of treating yourself, or use the self-treatment meditation that Usui Sensei taught, you should focus the energy on yourself on a regular basis to help bring things into balance for you on all levels, and to help you to release things that no longer serve you: mental states, emotions, physical things.

The energy will deal with many aspects of your body/mind, many deeply-embedded imbalances, if we give the energy the opportunity to do its work on us, digging deep and chipping away at the 'baggage' that we carry, over time.

We prefer to use Usui Sensei's self-treatment meditation because it seems more intense and versatile, but all self-treatment approaches are valid. Usui's Sensei's system was all about spiritual development and self-healing, so Hatsurei Ho and self-treatment can lie at the very heart of your Reiki practice.

You need to put yourself first, and the principle of kaizen means that by working on yourself consistently, great transformations are possible. You owe it to yourself to allow yourself to obtain the benefits that are available to you through Reiki.

Receive spiritual empowerments throughout your training and beyond.

Training with Usui was rather like martial arts training, where you were in ongoing contact with your teacher over an extended period of time. Part of your training involved receiving simple spiritual empowerments from Usui Sensei, repeatedly, at all levels.

Each empowerment reinforced your connection to the source, cleared your channel for the energy, allowed you to develop spiritually and enhanced your intuitive potential.

To echo this practice, Taggart sends out a distant Reiju empowerment every week, on a Monday, which can be 'tuned in to' by any Reiki person.

You can find out about this, and what to do, by visiting the Reiki Evolution web site.

On each occasion that you receive Reiju you are given what you need, and as your needs change from one occasion to another, this simple spiritual 'blessing' helps you to develop. A one-off attunement or empowerment does of course give you something permanent, and when you learn Reiki for the first time the attunements or empowerments that you receive provide you with the ability to use Reiki permanently, but it does not stop there: by receiving empowerments on a regular basis you are building momentum and allowing the energy to penetrate more deeply within you.

If we are committed to ongoing improvements within ourselves then we should make the time to receive an empowerment weekly. And again it is the regular commitment which is the key, the key to deepening your experience of the energy and its beneficial effects on you.

Work on developing your intuitive potential.

Mikao Usui's original system did not focus very much on the treatment of others, and any instruction on treatments would not have involved slavishly following a set of 'standard' hand positions that you had to apply to everyone you treated. Usui's method was simpler and more elegant. You allowed the energy to guide your hands to the right place to treat, different from one person to another, and different within the same person from one treatment to another.

The way we have been taught to do this is through a 'technique' called 'Reiji Ho' (indication of the spirit technique'), a way of emptying your mind and merging with the energy, getting your head out of the way to allow intuition to bubble to the surface.

The exciting thing about Reiji Ho is that it works for everyone, and with time - we come back to kaizen's small incremental improvements - your hands will move more quickly, more consistently, more effortlessly, and you will start to attract more intuitive information. So every time we treat someone we should spend time cultivating our 'Reiji' state of mind, and gradually, gradually, we develop.

Learn to become the energies.

…that you are introduced to at Second Degree and Master levels. Usui's system didn't involve symbols as far as most of his students were concerned. Students were expected to carry out meditations over an extended period of time in order to learn to experience different energies and, at Second Degree, students were introduced to the energies of "earth ki" and "heavenly ki", which represent two fundamental aspects of our being.

By practising 'becoming' earth ki and heavenly ki again and again – a powerful self-healing practice - these energies became so familiar to the students that they could 'connect' to the energy direct without having to use a prop like a symbol.

Usui provided some Shinto mantras for some of his students to use to invoke the energies, but it was possible to move beyond these mantras with time, too. In my article 'A Simple Way with Symbols' I describe a meditation that you can use to 'become' these energies.

But again we see that to obtain the greatest benefit, to enhance self-healing, to free up our practice and move beyond symbols, takes time and commitment. A quick meditation carried out a few times is not enough: Usui Sensei's students spent 6-9 months meditating on just one energy, and this was done because the principle of kaizen – plugging away and developing by small amounts again and again – led to deep changes over time.

Live your life according to Usui's guiding principles.

Usui's simple principles to live by offer perhaps the best example of the principle of kaizen in our Reiki practice: Usui Sensei's precepts are a work in progress. They are not something that you read through and think "OK, got that": the precepts are simple to read and understand but they are something that you drip-feed into your daily life over time, more and more over time.

We may begin by thinking about the precepts when we first come across them on a First Degree course: we reflect on how they might impinge on our lives, our thoughts and emotions, our behaviour; we might imagine situations from that past that might have proceeded better had we exemplified the precepts, and we might imagine situations in the future and see ourselves behaving in a way that demonstrates that we are living the precepts.

But this initial surge of interest in the precepts is not sufficient to produce the beneficial changes that the precepts can produce in our lives.

To fully embrace Usui Sensei's spiritual principles takes regular reflection and ongoing thought. On an ongoing basis we consider our thoughts and our behaviour, we reflect on the principles and what they mean to us.

If we do this then over time we will find that living the precepts becomes easier, that our behaviour is modifying itself, that there are more permanent changes in the way that we react and behave and relate to other people. But this will only happen if we 'chip away' at our current behaviour patterns, using the precepts as our guiding light. There are no quick fixes: the precepts are not just for First Degree. The precepts are the essence of our Reiki practice.

Now, we do not need to be perfect, we do not need to beat ourselves up for not applying each and every principle on all occasions, but by dedicating ourselves, and by forgiving ourselves, and by trying to do a little better each day than we did the day before, we transform ourselves.

That is the key to our kaizen of Reiki: dedication and commitment, patience and forgiveness, and openness to the source.

Long term.

Get out of the way!

In this short article I want to talk about the best way to approach working on other people, whether giving treatments or carrying out distant healing. I want to talk about our state of mind and our intent when channelling the energy.

The first thing I want to say is that we are just a channel for the energy, not the source of the energy. This seems an obvious thing to say, but we need to remember that we are not healers. We do not heal. We do not have that power.

What we do when we treat someone is simply to create a 'healing space' that the recipient can use to move more into a state of balance. The recipient is responsible for their own healing, for what they experience or don't experience; they are responsible for how they react to the treatment. They are healing themselves.

"Necessary bystanders"

We are just necessary bystanders in the process: we do not direct the energy and we do not determine the outcome.

So I am not so happy with the title "Reiki Healer" because it suggests that the Reiki practitioner has the power to heal; they do not. I don't think that the title "Reiki Necessary Bystander" is going to catch on, so I prefer to use the title "Reiki Practitioner". It describes what we do: we practise Reiki and it does not imply that we have the power to heal others.

This article is called "Get out of the way" because I believe that this is the best thing we can do when treating someone or when sending distant healing. We are not the source of the healing; we are not the source of the energy, so we do not need to be there, directing and controlling. We can stand aside and if we do so then the energy can flow strongly and clearly, without interference from us.

When we treat someone we are not 'cheerleading' for a particular end result: we do not give Reiki to get rid of someone's head ache, or back ache, or to resolve their Gall Bladder problem, though of course these things may result from channelling Reiki.

End results are out of our hands and to focus strongly on a particular purpose for the treatment is not helpful. Reiki will not be controlled by us in terms of end results and attempts to control the energy in this way just puts up barriers that prevent the energy from doing what it needs to do.

Rather like the well-meaning amateur who gets in the way and prevents the professional from doing their job properly, our attempts to focus the energy to produce a particular end result will hinder the process for the recipient.

Having a neutral intent

So our intent when treating someone or sending distant healing is that the energy should do whatever is appropriate for the recipient. We are neutral, we are detached, and we do not focus on outcomes. Ideally we should drift into a gentle meditative state when treating or sending distant healing, and this can be best achieved by our 'disappearing' into the energy, feeling ourselves merging with or becoming one with the energy.

We merge with the energy and we merge with the recipient; we are empty. We do by not doing.

Giving treatments while distracted

Though some people are taught that it is ok to talk and chat to people, or bystanders, when giving a Reiki treatment, to do such a thing is neither professional nor does it lead to effective treatments.

If we are distracted then the energy flows less strongly, so if we want to do the best for our clients then we need to keep quiet, and encourage the client to keep quiet too. You can try an experiment for yourself if you like, to prove to yourself that distraction lessens the strength of your Reiki.

You could try this at a Reiki share, for example. Start by resting your hands on someone's shoulders and allow the energy to flow for a while. Then deliberately start up a conversation with someone sitting near you: take your attention away from the recipient and fully engage in the conversation. Do this for a few minutes. Then bring your attention back to the recipient, be still and quiet, and allow the energy to flow. How has the recipient's experience of the energy varied?

Now, we do not need to be in a perfect meditative state in order to be an effective channel for Reiki, but it certainly helps to cultivate a still and empty mind. We are all human and it is perfectly normal for unwanted thoughts to appear in our head. But we should pay them no attention.

If we pay the unwanted thoughts attention and try to get rid of them we then have two lots of thoughts: the thoughts we did not want and all the new thoughts about the need to get rid of the first lot of thoughts. We have made things worse!

The best approach to unwanted thoughts, then, is to allow them to drift by like clouds: pay them no attention, do not engage with them. They will leave.

Some more may come, but pay them no attention either. In time you should find that your busy mind starts to quieten and some of your treatments will become beautiful meditations, with your mind emptying with the energy, and staying empty.

Some treatments will not be like this, of course, but we do not need to be perfect. We can cultivate a more meditative state over time, moving in the right direction, and without worrying too much about individual occasions when our untamed brain kept on talking to us. This is a work-in-progress!

So Reiki is simple: you empty your head, you merge with the energy, do you not direct, you do not control, you do not try; you empty yourself and merge with the recipient, standing aside to allow the energy do what it needs to do, without interference from us.

Reiki advice from Bruce Lee: Be like water

Excellent advice

"Be formless, shapeless… like water"

"True refinement seeks simplicity"

You might be surprised to hear that these words were spoken by Bruce Lee, film star and famous martial artist who developed Jeet Kune Do, a hybrid martial arts method that took the best approaches from different fighting systems and synthesised them into a flexible and effective fighting art.

Jeet Kune Do is referred to as a "style without style" where, unlike more traditional martial arts which Lee saw as rigid and formalistic, JKD is not fixed or patterned: it is more of a philosophy with guiding thoughts, a "style of no style". Bruce Lee often referred to JKD as "The art of expressing the human body" in his writings and in interviews.

And those comments got me wondering about Reiki, especially when Lee identified three different stages that someone's practice could go through.

He said that before training, people had a natural ability, something that was unformed and unfocused; training begins and the student learns how to follow the instruction, they are restricted to the framework that they are taught and many practitioners might not move beyond that stage, following the system almost by rote.

The third stage is where the practitioner moves beyond the rote learning to embrace simplicity and flexibility.

So how does that echo one's development with Reiki?

Well, before some people learn Reiki, they already have a healing ability, maybe unstructured or unconscious, unfocused, but a natural healing ability nevertheless. We have taught many such people, who have found that Reiki gives them a framework or a structure to work through, focusing and channelling and enhancing what they already had.

The student learns a particular approach, with some rules and standard hand positions and in some lineages quite a long list of things you can and can't, should and shouldn't, do with Reiki. Some practitioners remain at this stage, following the instructions they were given and remaining content with that way of working.

But you can move beyond that framework, simplifying your practice, altering what you do to the needs of the recipient.

You can embrace intuitive working, where you leave behind those basic rules to go 'freestyle' and, where Lee describes his system as "The art of expressing the human body", we could see intuitive working as "The art of expressing the energy".

Here we are empty and formless, flowing like water to where the water wants to go, joining with the energy and following it, directing the energy to where it wants to be directed, emphasising aspects of the energy that need to be emphasised.

We stand as a flexible conduit between the source and the recipient, empty, formless, fluid.

I believe that clutter-free Reiki is the best Reiki, and that by cutting away the rules and the dogma we can 'refine' (to use Lee's word) our Reiki practice.

Emptiness is the goal

Emptiness is the goal here: no planning, no thought about what you might do, just being there with the energy and the recipient; your treatment has no form, no structure and you simply follow the flow of energy, becoming the energy, merging with the recipient, with no expectations other than to just 'be'.

Over to you

Can you see Bruce Lee's description of advancement within martial arts in your own practice of Reiki?

Have you moved on from the basic procedures that you were taught, to find your own comfortable way with the energy?

Has Bruce Lee's advice that you should be "Be formless, shapeless… like water" and that "True refinement seeks simplicity" insinuated itself into the way that you practise Reiki now?

Simple energy exercises to get the energy flowing

In this post I'd like to share a couple of simple Reiki energy exercises that you can use to clear and cleanse, and balance your energy system. These exercises come from Original Japanese Reiki, were taught by Mikao Usui, and can be used every day.

They would be a lovely way to start your day, in fact.

The exercises are referred to as **kenyoku**, which means "dry bathing" and **joshin kokkyu ho**, which means something like "soul cleansing breathing method". You carry out the exercises in order, starting with a quick kenyoku and then moving on to a blissful experience when carrying out joshin kokkyu ho for several minutes.

Here's what to do:

Relax

Sit in a comfortable chair. Relax and close your eyes, and place your hands palms down on your lap.

Focus your attention on your Dantien point: an energy centre two fingerbreadths (3-5 cm) below your tummy button and 1/3 of the way into your body.

Say to yourself "I'm starting my energy exercises now".

Kenyoku

Kenyoku can be seen as a way of getting rid of negative energy.

Brush across your torso

Place the fingertips of your right hand near the top of the left shoulder, where the collarbone meets the bulge of the shoulder. The hand is lying flat on your chest. Draw your flat hand down and across the chest in a straight line, over the base of the sternum (where your breastbone stops and your abdomen starts, in the midline) and down to the right hip.

Exhale as you do this.

Do the same on the right side, using your left hand. Draw your left hand from the right shoulder, in a straight line across the sternum, to the left hip, and again exhale as you make the downward movement.

Do the same on the left side again (like you did at the start), so you will have carried out movements with your right hand, left hand, and right hand again.

Brush down your arms

Now put your right fingertips on the outer edge of the left shoulder, at the top of your slightly outstretched left arm, with your fingertips pointing sideways away from your body.

Move your right hand, flattened, along the outside of your arm, all the way to the fingertips and beyond, all the while keeping the left arm straight. Exhale as you do this.

Repeat this process on the right side, with the left hand placed on the right shoulder, and move it down the right arm to the fingertips and beyond. Exhale as you do this.

Repeat the process on the left side again, so you will have carried out movements with your right hand, left hand, and right hand again, like before.

Once you have carried out kenyoku, move straight on to joshin kokkyu ho.

Joshin kokkyu ho

Joshin kokkyu ho means 'Technique for Purification of the Spirit' or 'Soul Cleansing Breathing Method'. It is a meditation that focuses on the Dantien point.

Put your hands on your lap with your palms facing upwards and breathe naturally through your nose. Do not overbreathe: breathe naturally and gently.

Focus on your Dantien point and relax.

When you breathe in, visualise energy or light flooding into your crown chakra and passing into your Dantien and, as you pause before exhaling, feel that energy expand throughout your body, melting all your tensions.

When you breathe out, imagine that the energy floods out of your body in all directions as far as infinity.

Get into a nice gentle even rhythm of drawing the energy down, spreading it through your body, and flooding it out to the universe.

Do this for 10-15 minutes. You may feel energy/tingling in your hands and even in your feet, as the meditation progresses, but don't worry if you don't, because everyone is different.

Over to you

Carry out this sequence every day for a couple of weeks and notice what difference it makes to you in terms of:

- The strength of the energy
- Your sensitivity to the energy
- Your general contentment or demeanour

Have fun!

The simplest self-treatment meditation ever!

How were you taught to Self-Treat?

Most people who are taught Reiki will have been taught some form of self-treatment, a way of focusing the energy on yourself, for your own benefit, and the most common form of self-treatment is what I would refer to as a "Standard Western hands-on" self-treatment method.

This is where you rest your hands in a series of positions covering the head and torso and maybe beyond, and let the energy flow out of your hands into your body.

It works well, though some of the positions can often be uncomfortable to get to, or hold for any amount of time, and that can often detract from the blissfulness of the experience.

So what I'm going to talk about in a series of articles are "how to do Reiki on yourself" in a number of different ways, ways to Reiki self-treat that are perhaps different from what you have been taught.

And I'd like to start with what you might call "The simplest self-treatment method ever"!

Taggart's "Meditation with the intention to heal"

It is possible to self-treat without resting your hands on your body at all, using your intention or visualisation or pure intent. In this example, what you are doing is, basically, setting a definite intent and letting the energy do what it wants to do.

Here are some instructions:

- Make yourself comfortable in a seated position, maybe with your hands resting in your lap
- Close your eyes
- Start to become aware of your connection to the energy, your connection to Reiki
- Notice how that connection feels, with the energy engulfing you and building within you in just the right way for you in this moment
- As the energy flows, just remind yourself that your intention now is to heal, to heal on all levels, to rejuvenate, to rebalance
- Just say to yourself, "this is my time to heal now"
- And allow the energy to flow, to flow to wherever it needs to go to give you just what you need in this moment
- Stay in this safe space, allowing the energy to provide balance, and healing
- And finally bring yourself back when you feel ready, and open your eyes

So this method doesn't involve hand positions, or symbols, it doesn't require visualisation, it doesn't direct the energy in any way. You sit, you merge with the energy and you allow it to flow, to do what it needs to do.

And you can just be there as a bystander in the process, observing, experiencing, in a neutral way: merged with the energy.

Over to you

If this self-treatment method is new to you, why not give it a try?

Intuitive self-healing meditation

Taggart's "Intuitive self-healing meditation"

This is still a very simple self-treatment method, where you're not resting your hands on yourself, but allowing the self-healing to occur through meditating.

What is new in this meditation is that we are going is to notice where the energy is flowing, and we are going to focus our attention on those areas.

Here's what to do.

- Make yourself comfortable in a seated position, maybe with your hands resting in your lap, and close your eyes
- Start to become aware of your connection to the energy, your connection to Reiki
- Notice how that connection feels, with the energy engulfing you and building within you in just the right way for you in this moment
- As the energy flows, just remind yourself that your intention now is to heal, to heal on all levels, to rejuvenate, to rebalance
- Just say to yourself, "this is my time to heal now"
- And allow the energy to flow, to flow to wherever it needs to go to give you just what you need in this moment
- *And start to become aware of the energy and where it's flowing*
- *Where is the Reiki focusing itself, where is it dwelling?*
- *Allow your attention to rest on that area; bring your awareness there*

- *If the energy moves on to another area, bring your attention to that new area, and notice the energy there*
- Stay in this safe space, allowing the energy to provide balance, and healing
- And finally bring yourself back when you feel ready, and open your eyes

So this method doesn't involve hand positions, or symbols, it doesn't require visualisation, it doesn't direct the energy in any way. You sit, you merge with the energy and you allow it to flow, to do what it needs to do.

What is different, though, is your attention: you follow the flow of energy and wherever the energy is directing itself, you focus your attention there too.

This is a powerful thing to do because where you focus your attention is where the energy focuses itself.

By allowing your attention to rest on the areas of need, you intensify and boost the flow of energy because "where thought goes, energy flows".

And you can just be there as a bystander in the process, observing, experiencing, in a neutral way: merged with the energy and following the flow of energy.

Over to you

If this self-treatment method is new to you, why not give it a try?

Mikao Usui's original self-treatment meditation

In my last article I described my "intuitive Reiki self-healing meditation" where you followed the flow of energy and focused your attention on the areas where the energy wanted to go.

This was a beneficial practice because resting your attention somewhere helps to boost the flow of Reiki, making the treatment more intense and focused in the areas that your attention is dwelling on.

So now we can build on the idea of the energy focusing itself where your attention is dwelling, by carrying out a meditation where you allow your attention to rest on five different areas of the head, spending a few minutes focusing on each position. This is a self-treatment method taught by Reiki's founder, Mikao Usui.

The Usui self-treatment meditation

Here's what to do.

- Make yourself comfortable in a seated position, maybe with your hands resting in your lap, and close your eyes
- Start to become aware of your connection to the energy, your connection to Reiki
- Notice how that connection feels, with the energy engulfing you and building within you in just the right way for you in this moment
- As the energy flows, just remind yourself that your intention now is to heal, to heal on all levels, to rejuvenate, to rebalance
- Just say to yourself, "this is my time to heal now"

- ***Allow your attention to focus on your forehead, by the hairline, and allow the energy to dwell there, building, intensifying***
- *Move your attention so you focus on your temples, on both sides of your head at the same time*
- *Move your attention so that you focus on the back of the head, and on the forehead, those two areas at the same time*
- *Move your focus so your attention comes to rest on the back of your neck, the base of your skull*
- *Move your attention to the crown, the crown of your head, focus your attention there*
- *And finally bring yourself back when you feel ready, and open your eyes*

So this method doesn't involve physical hand positions, or symbols, and it doesn't necessarily require visualisation either, because while you might choose to imagine that there are hands treating those areas, you can just as simple allow your attention to rest on those areas and the energy will flow there.

In each position, you merge with the energy and you allow it to flow, to do what it needs to do.

What is different about this meditation, though, is your attention: you direct the flow of energy by focus your attention on a particular area. This is a powerful thing to do because where you focus your attention is where the energy focuses itself.

By allowing your attention to rest on the areas of need, you intensify and boost the flow of energy because "where thought goes, energy flows".

And you can just be there as a bystander in the process, observing, experiencing, in a neutral way: merged with the energy and following the flow of energy.

Over to you

If this self-treatment method is new to you, why not give it a try?

Intuitive hands-on self-treatment method

In previous articles I have been talking about meditative approaches to self-treatment, where you either:

- Meditate with the intention to heal… and just let it happen
- Follow the flow of energy and focus your attention on where the energy is focusing itself
- Direct the flow of energy by resting your attention on different areas of the body

Now I'm going to turn my attention to hands-on self-treatments, but with a bit of a twist. Out go standard self-treatment hand-positions and in comes…

Taggart's Intuitive hands-on self-treatment method

- Make yourself comfortable in a seated or supine position, maybe with your hands folded over each other in front of your chest
- Close your eyes
- Start to become aware of your connection to the energy, your connection to Reiki
- Notice how that connection feels, with the energy engulfing you and building within you in just the right way for you in this moment
- As the energy flows, just remind yourself that your intention now is to heal, to heal on all levels, to rejuvenate, to rebalance
- Just say to yourself, "this is my time to heal now"
- And allow the energy to flow, to flow to wherever it needs to go to give you just what you need in this moment

- *And start to become aware of the energy and where it's flowing*
- *Where is the Reiki focusing itself, where is it dwelling?*
- *Move your hands to rest on, or near, that area*
- **Allow your hands to drift to the best place for them to be**
- *Stay in that position for as long as you need to*
- *If the energy moves on to another area, if your hands want to move on to another area, let that happen*
- *Allow the energy to guide you*
- *And finally bring yourself back when you feel ready, and open your eyes*

Although this method involves resting your hands on your body – whereas in all the previous self-treatment examples I gave you, you were simply meditating – there are no expectations here.

You rest your hands, and move your hands, according to your individual energy needs during each session.

Each treatment you carry out will most likely be different in some way, as your energy needs vary from one occasion to another.

You might be following the energy, noticing where it wants to flow, and moving your hands to a suitable nearby area.

Or you might find that the hands start to move and drift by themselves, again guided by the energy, giving you exactly what you need on each occasion.

Over to you

If this self-treatment method is new to you, why not give it a try?

The simplest hands-on self-treatment method ever

This is the final article in the series, so I thought I would finish by a very simple hands-on method…

Just rest your hands on yourself and close your eyes

That's it.

That's the method.

Rest your hands on your heart and solar plexus, close your eyes, and let the Reiki flow.

Or rest your hands on your lower abdomen, like in the photo above.

Bliss out on the energy.

Let it go where it wants to go and do what it wants to do.

And when you're done, open your eyes.

Over to you

If this self-treatment method is new to you, why not give it a try?

The "21 Day" thing

Where did the 21 day thing come from?

I wanted to talk a little bit about the "21 day thing": the 21-day self-treat or the 21-day clear-out after attending a First Degree course.

I'm a bit puzzled by this and I've been trying to fathom where it came from, and why it should be recommended.

I think this idea probably came into being because it echoes the story told about Mikao Usui's discovery of Reiki on Mt Kurama where, according to the story that Mrs Takata passed on, Usui Sensei went up Mt Kurama and fasted and meditated for 21 days, culminating in him being hit by a bolt of light, seeing symbols, and Reiki was born.

We know now that this isn't actually what happened: Usui didn't fast for 21 days up the mountain, though he did carry out something called the "Lotus Repentance meditation", and this did last for 21 days I believe.

But this was quite a formalised process – an established Tendai practice – and he went home at night after each day's meditation. In any case, this did not lead to the 'eureka' moment that Mrs Takata spoke about since Usui was already teaching his system before he carried out the first of his Lotus Repentance meditations, and he performed these meditations several times during his lifetime.

7 x 3 = 21

People have speculated and taught that the 21 consecutive days of self-treating is required because the energy makes a visit to each of a person's chakras three times during this period.

The emphasis on chakras within Reiki seems to have originated within Reiki's journey through the New Age movement, where some lineages have incorporated various New Age practices like crystals, spirit guides and Angels etc. Chakra work wasn't part of the original system.

And this three-times-through-your-chakras seems to me to be a bit of 'reverse engineering', where you have something that you're supposed to do, and then you backtrack to try and find a justification for it, to make sense of it in your head.

Some suggest that if you carry out a practice for 21 days then you will have established it as a habit, and there may be something in that, actually.

Don't stop after 21 days!

The problem that I have with this idea of a 21-day practice is that some people "do their 21 days" and then stop, or have only a sporadic practice afterwards, as if once you've done your 21 days… that's it, you've cleared yourself out and you don't need to work on yourself so dedicatedly afterwards.

And I also have a problem with the idea that you have a clear-out just during that 21 day period and then you're sorted.

In my experience, the way that people react to Reiki in terms of 'clearing out', whether that be in terms of physical reactions or states of mind or emotions, seems to vary greatly from one person to another. And while Reiki doesn't seem to give people an experience that they can't handle, some can make a great big fast clear-out initially, some have it happening in dribs and drabs, while for others the process may be delayed for a while.

Everyone's different. And there's always something more to clear out!

We all live lives, we have stress, we suppress emotions, we fail to deal with things, so if we carry on working with Reiki, there will be stuff that we will need to shift in the future to bring things into balance for us, not just in those first few weeks.

And just wait until you start attuning people: you may have a mega-clear-out waiting for you!

So while I don't object to people working on themselves dedicatedly for three weeks – why would I? – I'd rather emphasise that if you're going to gain the greatest benefit out of your connection to Reiki then you need to work on yourself regularly.

You don't have to self-treat (or carry out Hatsurei ho) **every** single day (and then beat yourself up for not being perfect if you have to miss a day sometimes) but if you can make Reiki a regular part of your life then you will reap the rewards.

And that's not just for 21 days: that's for life.

Over to you

So, do you have a regular practice of using Reiki on yourself?

And, if so, what have you noticed in terms of the way that your mind/body has responded to that ongoing energy work?

Did you have a bit of a clear-out to begin with, or a great big clear-out, and then occasional ups and downs after then?

Your 10 day Reiki challenge: the "Releasing Exercise"

What is the Releasing Exercise?

I love the way that the Reiki precepts, and the effects of learning Reiki, blend and merge with each other. So if you could encapsulate in words the effects of Reiki on a person, you would probably say that they were largely free from anger and worry and that they were more mindful.

And at the same time we have a set of precepts that encourage us to be mindful, and to let go of worry and anger.

Mikao Usui's precepts are such an important part of the original system and something that can sometimes become overlooked during the head-long rush to get to all the cool energy stuff! But they are really the foundation of Reiki, there to guide us and also to represent and give form to the many changes that Reiki can bring us.

And that got me thinking about whether there was a way of actually using the energy of Reiki to directly experience a precept.

What I came up with was my "Releasing Exercise".

The Releasing Exercise is a way of directly experiencing the effects of a precept in terms of energy flow and the people that I have shared this with have found it to be very powerful.

Maybe you'll find it powerful too.

I am setting you a challenge: to carry out my Releasing Exercise each day for 10 days.

How to perform the Releasing Exercise

I would like to suggest that you do the following, for a couple of minutes at a time, twice a day, for ten days: Sit with your eyes closed and your hands resting in your lap, palms up. You are going to be releasing energy through your hands.

Stage One

Sit comfortably with your eyes closed and your hands resting in your lap, palms up. Take a few long deep breaths and feel yourself becoming peaceful and relaxed. Your mind empties. Say to yourself "I now release all my anger…"; say this three times to yourself if you like. Allow energy to be released through your palms, and be still until the flow of energy subsides. This may take a little while, particularly the first time you try this exercise.

Stage Two

Now say to yourself "I now release all my worry…"; say this three times to yourself if you like. Again allow a flurry of energy to leave your hands and be still until it subsides. Again this may take a little while, particularly the first time you try this exercise.

Try this variation

I really like this variation: try carrying out the releasing exercise in time with your breath. Breathe in gently, say to yourself "I now release all my anger…" and then breathe out, allowing your anger to flood out of you on the out breath, flooding out of your palms. Gently breathe in, and repeat.

Let Taggart Talk You Through It

If you'd like me to talk you through the exercise, go to the Reiki Evolution blog and search for 'releasing exercise'. You'll find an audio track there.

Here's what people experienced

I have included some representative feedback below, so you can see the sort of thing that the exercise has done for people.

Here's what I received from Loretta in Iowa, who has started to use the exercise with her clients:

"I use the release in the morning as I lay in Relaxation pose after finishing yoga and when I feel an emotion I need to work with during the day. I use it for more than anger and worries and the feeling leaving my hands is very emotional. I have also begun using in it in my Reiki practice. I take my clients through breathing exercises and relaxation steps and depending on what is going on with them I introduce the releasing exercise either before the Reiki session or at the end of the session.

Practicing the release is so healing on many levels, it allows us to focus on one issue at a time, allows us to take time for ourself, to dig deep on issues we may want to push to the background. This process makes my day wonderful, I feel so much more on an even keel with the world and with myself."

Emma in Scotland has experimented with the exercise, focusing the energy on releasing other emotions:

"I have tried the 10 day releasing exercise and found it really beneficial – I'm going to continue doing it everyday. It's really effective and so simple! I have a lot of bottled up

emotion and I feel much more relaxed after doing this and feel quite a powerful flow of energy leaving my body.

I have tried other variations which also seem to work such as saying "I release sadness" or "regret" or sometimes even "I release any unnecessary or unhelpful emotion". I even tried it lying down imagining the energy flowing out through the soles of my feet so that I could do it last thing at night before going to sleep. I'm not sure that's as effective but I did feel relaxed! Anyway, thank you for the idea and I will continue to use it."

Here's what I received from Vivien in the UK, who found the exercise worked well when dealing with a difficult issue that arose:

"Well your exercises arrived at a very good time for me. We had a very difficult "political/social" issue at work whereby I got so angry (on someone else's behalf). This person had offloaded her problems to me and I was surprised how angry I felt inside at the injustice that she had suffered. It was one of those situations I took home with me.

I did offer her advice and suggested various courses of action which helped her but, despite that, I still had this real burning anger inside me which I took home with me on a Friday. I did your 'anger releasing' exercises on the Friday and over the weekend and it certainly helped! I practiced it a few times each day and hey presto, I was chilled by the Monday and everything has now been resolved thankfully!

I didn't need to do it for 10 days but in future if I find myself in a similar situation, I will know what to do. I will also try out the others. So a big thank you!!!!"

Teresa in the UK sent me her feedback, and she found that the exercise helped her to just 'be':

"This is a wonderful exercise for letting go of anger and worry. The more I practised this the more I became lighter and freer in my thoughts and actions. Being in the present, no past, no future, simply alive in the moment.

Thank you very much for this."

Paul from the UK contacted me to say that the exercise helped to change his perception of things:

"I'm very new to Reiki and started your releasing exercise as another "string to my bow". Before starting my Reiki journey, I was already practicing mindful meditation. I've found your release exercise a natural extension of this.

I work in a quite highly stressed office environment, a place where small irritations can rapidly grow into something more. I'm generally very relaxed and laid back anyway, but over the last ten days my colleagues have seen fit to comment about how even MORE laid back I seem to have become.

I've been self-reflecting on this. At first I thought the exercise was helping me become more tolerant, but I now realise that's not the case at all. "Tolerance" is more about "putting up with the irritation". I think I would say I now have more "acceptance". Because I'm free from anger and worry, I can "accept" things that would have been seen as irritants. Because I "accept" them, I don't have to "tolerate" them.

I've passed your exercise to a number of my Reiki friends who expressed an interest. I'm waiting to hear back from them."

Pat explained how the exercise has helped her with two specific situations recently:

"I started the releasing exercise before Chistmas and have found it very effective. I felt the release of energy in my palms and very often in my third eye area. I sometimes felt warmth, almost like a hot flush!!!

Two things happened during the time that I was doing the exercise which would have normally been very upsetting under normal circumstances but I dealt with it using this practice. I have tried both ways of the practice as you suggested and they were both equally effective.

The first situation that I mentioned above was a very cutting comment made by someone which was hurtful and as soon as it happened, I did the release exercise and the effect was very comforting. The second was some health news that made me angry and concerned. I again used the practice to release the anger, worry and blame. I found the exercise very helpful in both of those situations.

I have continued to do the practice and yesterday started to add fear as well as anger and worry to my routine. I will definitely continue with this exercise. I am very grateful to you and thank you very much for telling us about this."

Finally, Marilynne explains how she feels that this exercise is very much in line with the way that we do things at Reiki Evolution:

"I have not done the releasing exercise regularly over 10 days. However when I do use it, it is very effective in releasing thoughts of both worry and anger, the two detrimental, mischievous little devils that can be so disruptive in their negativity. I cherish the precepts and accept them as powerful ideals and daily reminders. I have just had my Reiki 2 session last weekend and feel the energy so much stronger now through my hand and down

to the tan-den. The releasing exercise seems so natural, and very much 'in tune' with all that I have learned and experienced through Reiki Evolution. Practicing control of the flow of Reiki energy, including the release of worry and anger, is just a wonderful privilege."

Time For You To Take The 10 Day Releasing Exercise Challenge!

So now it's over to you: your turn to carry out my releasing exercise for ten days, if you want to!

Using Reiki for anxiety

Does Reiki work for Anxiety?

I think a lot of people come to Reiki wondering if it can help ease their anxiety, and I think that there is a general sense that Reiki can help you to become more calm and chilled. So is Reiki good for anxiety? Will it help you to let go of those worries?

Well in my experience, yes, Reiki does really work to help reduce anxiety and there are three ways that it does this, I think.

1. Through mindfulness
2. Through the use of the Reiki precepts
3. Through meditating on and using the Reiki energy

What is Anxiety?

When we worry, we are thinking about the future and what might happen to us or the people we care about. We imagine a frightening or unhappy future and that makes us scared.

And since we have fairly prehistoric brains and responses, we respond to this future threat like it was some sort of sabre-toothed tiger in front of us: we go into 'flight, fright or freeze' mode, with elevated heart rate, high blood pressure and the like.

Long term, this is not good for our bodies since our immune system is dampened down and blood is rerouted away from our digestive systems, so we end up run down, prone to infection and with digestive disturbances.

All because we are responding to an imaginary future.

How can Reiki help Anxiety?

There are two important aspects of Reiki training that work together to ease anxiety: mindfulness and the Reiki precepts I'm not going to go into detail about these in this article, since I have spoken about them elsewhere, but these two aspects of Reiki training very much work with each other to reduce anxiety.

The Reiki precepts start with the phrase "just for today" and that emphasises the idea of mindfulness, where you are fully immersed in the moment, fully engaged with what you are doing. "Just for today" exhorts us, just for this moment, to be content, to be compassionate and forgiving of ourselves, to be aware of the many blessings that we have in our lives.

If you are mindful then there are no thoughts about the past or the future: you are embracing the present moment, and when you do this it's not easy to worry (because you can only do this when you send yourself off into an imagined negative future).

Although mindfulness isn't emphasised or even mentioned on a lot of Reiki courses, it is an important part of the original system that Mikao Usui taught and is something that we explain and encourage as soon as you start your Reiki training with us.

Reiki energy and Anxiety

But beyond the practice of mindfulness, and the benefits that come when introducing the Reiki principles into your daily life, there is something else going on too. because when you are 'connected' to Reiki, when you are aware of and working with the energy through daily energy exercises and meditations, changes take place within you that very much echo the benefits of mindfulness and precepts-work.

Reiki, in itself – Reiki, the energy – helps people to feel more calm, content and serene, better able to cope with difficult situations and people. Working with Reiki helps you to come back into contact with that core part of you that is balanced and centred, a still foundation that can weather the storms that life often throws at us.

Do you already have Reiki?

If so, and if you feel that there is still a bit more work to be done in terms of leaving worry behind, there are a couple of techniques I created that I think will be of great help to you. You can read about them in other articles. Here are the titles:

- Releasing exercise
- Precepts rehearsal

These exercises allow you to use the Reiki energy as a 'carrier' to disperse or dissipate any accumulated worry, and also help you to set a new course, so you respond differently in the future. These exercises are deceptively powerful and should be carried out for several weeks to gain the full benefit from them.

Using Reiki for stress

Can Reiki help with Stress?

In my last article I was talking about how Reiki can help with Anxiety and while stress and anxiety are often lumped together as if they were the same things, there is quite a difference between these two experiences in terms of what's going on.

Where anxiety is a fear of an imagined future, where you feel frightened about things that are yet to happen and may not actually happen, with stress you are reflecting on how you believe you're going to be able to cope with different tasks or events. Stress is all about "I can't do this", "I'm not going to be able to do this".

So stress is all about how competent you believe you are and becoming frightened about letting yourself down, or letting other people down. Stress is about losing face, not succeeding in a particular task or goal, it's about fear of showing that you're not good enough.

Using Reiki for Stress relief

So **can Reiki help with stress** and, if so, how does that happen?

Well, I think it comes down to the three powerful aspects of the Reiki that we introduce to students on our First Degree courses: mindfulness, the Reiki precepts and regular energy work.

I'm not going to go into a lot of detail about mindfulness because I have written about it before, but when you are mindful you are fully engaged in and engrossed with the task at hand, whether that doing the washing up or going for a walk. You become fully aware of the experience of you doing the task, living fully in the present moment, with no thoughts of the future or the past.

You might notice the flow of energy through your nostrils, the feeling in the soles of your feet as you walk, the sounds of birdsong, the myriad of colours that are before you, the sensation of soap suds on your fingertips, the swishing of the water. You notice your thoughts pass by like clouds.

In doing so you start to come into contact with a still, calm centre that we all have within us if we give ourselves a chance to experience it, that place from which we can observe, non-judgmentally.

It is in this still place where we can let go of those feelings of stress, setting us free, and the more we practise mindfulness, the more often and more easily can we ease into that helpful state.

The Reiki precepts and stress

The Reiki precepts (or the Reiki principles, or 'Gokai') are a simple set of 'rules to live by' that were established and taught by Reiki's founder, Mikao Usui. There were said to distil the essence of Tendai Buddhist teachings into a simple set of guiding principles that anyone can follow.

The Reiki precepts emphasise humility and compassion: compassion for ourselves as much as compassion for others. So how can we be compassionate towards ourselves and how can that help with stress?

Well, we can forgive ourselves, we can give ourselves a break and forgive ourselves for not being perfect. If we expect ourselves to be perfect then no matter how hard we work, no matter how much we achieve, no matter what we do or try to do, we will never be happy.

So we can give ourselves some self-love and understanding, we can nurture ourselves, and the best place from which to do this is from that still, calm centre that we gain a glimpse of when we are mindful.

Reiki energy and Stress

Tying these strands together – the mindfulness and the compassion and self-forgiveness – is the use of Reiki energy on ourselves.

By having a good, regular routine of working on ourselves using Reiki – by carrying out daily energy exercises and some form of self-treatment – we nudge our energy system more into a state of balance, bathing us in calm, helping us to fully experience that content, still core, and putting us in the best possible position to really benefit from this wonderful system.

Oh, and I just wanted to mention that although in this article I am talking about learning Reiki as a way of managing your stress, receiving Reiki treatments on a regular basis is also a wonderful way of experiencing the powerful balancing effect of this simple hands-on therapy.

Can you send distant healing at Reiki first degree?

An unnecessary piece of dogma

It is taught commonly on Reiki courses that you aren't able to do distant healing at First Degree and that you can only send distant healing once you've been 'attuned' to the distant healing symbol.

I don't agree with that and think it's unnecessarily dogmatic and limiting... and makes no sense!

Firstly, distant healing isn't something that is unique to Reiki: many spiritual healers practise this. So we have a group of people who haven't been attuned to Reiki at all, they haven't been 'attuned' to anything in a Reiki sense, and they can send distant healing.

So are we saying that people who haven't been attuned to Reiki are able to send distant healing, but once you're attuned to First Degree then this ability somehow stops, only to start again when you've been on a Second Degree course?

That makes no sense!

And let's think about the Buddhist origins of Reiki: one of the principles of Buddhism is that reality is illusion, the idea of us being separate individuals, distinct from other people, is illusion, and that the true reality is that of oneness.

Mikao Usui was a Buddhist.

Mainly, he taught people who were Buddhists or followers of Shinto.

Would he have established an energetic system, when his whole worldview was based on the idea of oneness, that suddenly went against this grain and introduced the idea that people at First Degree were in some way exempt from this basic Buddhist principle of oneness?

I don't think so.

Distant Healing at First Degree

So we teach the basics of distant healing on our First Degree course, and why wouldn't we, since it's an essential part of the energy system that we use. We teach a simple approach, but it doesn't need to be complicated.

We don't teach the 'distant healing symbol' (referred to as 'HSZSN') on First Degree and we don't need to because you don't need to use that symbol, or be 'attuned' to it, in order to send distant healing effectively.

When we do teach the distant healing symbol on Second Degree, certainly it does provide a useful focus, though to be honest I prefer to use the corresponding kotodama instead since I believe that this mantra helps to make connections on a whole new level, whether working on someone in person or at a distance.

Experiment

If you're currently at First Degree, why not experiment with distant healing and see what's possible.

To get you started if you're not sure what to do, take a look at the article called "The simplest distant healing method ever!": anyone can use it; it's symbol free and it works well.

At Reiki Evolution we're happy for our students to experiment and find their own way with the energy: we don't want out students to turn into clones of us!

Restrictions on Reiki

Depending on whom you trained with, you may have been given quite a long list of 'situations where you should not use Reiki'. It seems that the only restriction that Mrs Takata taught was that you should not treat a broken bone with Reiki, but many other restrictions have been added in later on in Reiki's Western history. I thought I would spend a little time talking about these 'Reiki contraindications'.

The "broken bone" thing

Firstly, I would like to talk about the 'broken bone' restriction. This is made on the basis that Reiki accelerates the healing process, so you do not want Reiki to set the bone before it has been put back in the right position.

Now while Reiki is an amazing energy, and has done some wonderful and breathtaking things, I think most people's experience is that Reiki gently supports the body's natural healing ability, and that while it may accelerate the healing process, the effects of Reiki generally build up cumulatively. I do not believe that Reiki will set someone's bone like fast-acting Polyfilla, so that they will have to have the bone re-broken and re-set when they get to Casualty a few hours later.

Breaking a bone is a shocking and painful experience (I know this from first hand experience!) and Reiki could make a real difference to someone, so I would not hold back from giving it, and I would not hold back from treating the area where the bone is broken.

Suggesting that you could Reiki someone, but keep well away from the broken bone, does not stop Reiki from rushing to where it is needed (the bone), and why would we imagine that what many people see as a spiritually-guided life-force energy would mess things up for a person. Reiki is supposed to be intelligent.

Reiki and pacemakers

Another situation where some people are taught that you 'should not treat' is when a client has a pacemaker. This restriction is made on the basis that Reiki energy is electromagnetic in nature, and will interfere with the proper functioning of the device.

Confusingly, some say that this restriction only applies to analogue pacemakers, not the newer digital ones.

There seems to be no evidence whatsoever to indicate that Reiki would cause a problem in this area, and I have not heard on a single anecdote where a Reiki practitioner treated someone with a pacemaker and the treatment caused problems.

I am also not aware of any evidence to show that Reiki is electromagnetic in nature, either. If it was, you could measure Reiki easily: move your hand over a wire and you would induce an electric current, which you could pick up with a voltmeter.

Some have suggested that you can solve this 'problem' by keeping away from the heart area, but we all know that Reiki rushes from where we put it to where it is needed.

I would have thought that a person with a pacemaker needed more Reiki in the heart area, not less, and if Reiki is drawn to the areas of need then it is going to go where it wants anyway. The only solution would be not to treat someone with a pacemaker, which I think is ridiculous.

Some have suggested that you should not attune someone with a pacemaker, and again I do not think that this is sensible. I am not going to restrict my practice of Reiki on the basis of unfounded supposition.

Where is the evidence?

With nearly all the restrictions that are put on Reiki, there seems to be no evidence to back up any of them. I am not talking about double blind clinical trials here, but even simple anecdotes where a practitioner has treated someone and found that there is a problem that can be reasonably attributed to the treatment that has been given.

I have heard that you should not treat insulin-dependent Diabetics, or people taking steroids for adrenal insufficiency. Those restrictions have been made on the basis that if Reiki produces an instant cure then the patient's next dose of insulin, or steroids, will kill them.

Again, while Reiki is a wonderful healing force, it is not my belief that Reiki is likely to cure diabetes, for example, at the click of a finger.

Most people's experience is that the effects of Reiki build up cumulatively and that if a condition has taken a long time to develop, then it is not so likely to disappear straight away. Yes, a diabetic patient's blood glucose levels may vary after a Reiki treatment, but diabetics' blood sugar levels vary a great deal anyway. That is why they have to keep on sticking themselves with a pin to monitor their levels, and you could only attribute this variation to Reiki if it happened consistently after treatments and their blood sugar levels were stable the rest of the time.

Having said that, there does seem to be some anecdotal evidence that Reiki treatments can sometimes cause the client's blood sugar levels to alter after a treatment. This does not mean that you should not treat diabetics: it means that you need to keep this in mind and mention this possibility to the client, so that they can monitor their blood sugar levels accordingly.

Waking up and falling asleep

I have heard that you should not send distant Reiki to someone who is driving a car, because they will fall asleep, and you should not send distant Reiki to someone who is under an anaesthetic, because it will make them wake up... well, which is it? This doesn't sound like an intelligent energy to me, and there seems to be a lot of fear, and a lack of trust in the energy, underlying all these restrictions.

So where is the evidence that Reiki wakes people up during surgery? Where is even one anecdote where it was clear that Reiki, rather than any other cause, led to this happening?

Look for the evidence, and you find that these scare stories have no foundation.

Cancer, pregnancy, depression, asthma, stress, homoeopathy, animals, medicines

In fact, the restrictions do not stop there. There are many more taught in different lineages. For example, you should not treat people with cancer, you should not treat people who are pregnant, you should not treat people who are depressed or who have asthma, you should not treat people who are stressed, you should not treat young children, you should not treat animals, you should not treat people who are taking homoeopathic remedies, you should not treat people who are taking medicines, you should not treat people wearing green trousers (sorry, I made that one up!).

Let's just examine two of these. It is said by some teachers that you should not treat people who have cancer because

Reiki will "feed the cancer"; there is a variation on this myth, actually, where people are taught that they should not use one of the Reiki symbols because it will "put energy into the cancer".

Let's think rationally about this for just a second: we have cancer cells inside us all of the time and as you sit reading this, there are cancer cells in you. Your cells go haywire all the time and your immune system detects the errors and kills the cells. But if you adhere to this Reiki contraindication then you should not treat anyone at all because Reiki feeds cancer cells, and everyone has cancer cells in them, so we can't treat people, or animals, we can't treat ourselves, and being attuned would be a death sentence!

And if we can't treat pregnant women then we really need to refrain from treating any women of childbearing age because of course women can be in the early stages of pregnancy and not know about it, or be pregnant and not know about it. And then of course all women of childbearing age should refrain from self-treating, and should not go on Reiki courses.

People do not think things through.

I believe that Reiki is a beautiful healing energy that supports the body's natural healing ability, and brings things into balance on all levels. It either has an innate intelligence, and knows where to go to an extent, or it is the body that is intelligent and draws the energy to where it is needed.

In either case, Reiki is not going to mess up a person and leave them less well off than they were before they started, other than a temporary intensification of symptoms.

Examples of these would be an emotional release or strong emotions felt for a few days after being treated, or joint pains getting worse during a treatment and then improving subsequently.

Distant healing

The last set of restrictions that I have heard about concern distant healing, where it is said in some quarters that you should not send Reiki to people who have not asked for or given their permission.

Some people say that it is totally unethical to send distant Reiki to someone without obtaining their agreement and that it a gross intrusion. I do not agree with this, for a number of reasons:

1. Firstly, I see sending distant Reiki as rather like sending concentrated prayer. When you pray for someone you are asking for Divine intervention in another person's life, in whatever way is right for that person according to Divine will. You are asking for things to change for the better. When you send Reiki you are sending it with loving intent and for the person's highest good, so it is in line with that person's destiny or karma, and many people see Reiki energy as having Divine origins. You do not ring someone up to ask their permission to pray for them, so why should if be different with Reiki?
2. If someone were knocked over by a car a few yards away from you, would you really not send Reiki to them because you couldn't drag them into the seated position to sign a consent form? No. You would send Reiki to their highest good and let the energy do what is appropriate for them. You offer the energy: you do not force the recipient to receive it.
3. Reiki is a beautiful healing energy that brings things into balance on all levels and does not mess people up, leaving them worse off than they were to begin with. With distant healing your intent is that the

energy works for the highest good of the recipient, so if it is not appropriate for that person to get the benefit of the energy then it simply will not work. You are not imposing your will and you are not imposing your preferred solution on the situation. You are simply sending love, offering the energy, making the energy available, not forcing it to be received.

For these reasons, I have no problem in sending Reiki to people who have not specifically requested it. I send the energy with the intention that it be received by the recipient at whatever time is appropriate for them.

I do not see that there are any other restrictions that need to be applied to the energy, or the practice of Reiki.

In the West we think too much, and come up with too many complications. Reiki is simple and does not need to be restricted.

It knows what to do.

Intelligent Energy?

It is well established within Reiki that the energy we channel is 'intelligent'. Some people believe that the energy is innately intelligent, perhaps because of its divine origins, and some believe that the intelligence of the energy is accounted for by the presence of spirit guides who direct the energy as we treat someone.

Others believe that it is the body that is intelligent, drawing the energy to where it needs to go.

Most of us will have noticed that the energy will move from where our hands are resting to other parts of the recipient's body, drawn according to the recipient's need to areas of need, so it is clear that it doesn't always restrict itself to where we place it.

Some people take the line that Reiki will work perfectly well no matter what hand positions you use, irrespective of the knowledge and experience of the practitioner and whether or not the practitioner can work intuitively.

The implication of this is that you could quite happily carry out a Reiki treatment by simply holding someone's hands for an hour and the energy would be drawn to the areas of need, and that there is nothing that you could do to help make the treatment more effective.

Another view is that there are things that a practitioner can do in order to increase the effectiveness of a treatment, for example:

- Working on yourself to develop your ability as a channel
- Using intuition to decide where to put your hands (rather than following standard hand positions) and

what aspect of the energy to emphasise during the treatment, or where to direct your attention.

There are some inconsistencies in the first view described above. Many people will use techniques designed to balance the chakras, while at the same time maintaining that Reiki is intelligent and will always give the recipient what they need. Yet imposing your will on the energy and using it to balance the chakras is over-riding the way that the energy will work in the body, is it not?

Surely if Reiki is an intelligent energy then it will balance the recipient's chakras in a way that is appropriate for the individual, without the practitioner doing anything specific to achieve this.

If you routinely direct Reiki to balance a person's chakras you are suggesting that Reiki will not balance the chakras without direct intervention by the practitioner. Since most people would agree that Reiki works on your energy system and produces beneficial effects on all levels, how could it not balance your chakras during this process?

Either Reiki is intelligent, in which case you don't need to spend time balancing people's chakras, or it isn't intelligent, in which case we would always need to move in to balance the chakras.

But if Reiki can't even balance your chakras on its own, what on earth is it doing?

I believe that spending time balancing people's chakras using Reiki is unnecessary, and that Reiki will do to a person's chakras what needs to be done to achieve balance for them at the end of a treatment.

Of course subsequently the chakras will drift out of balance again, back to their more habitual state, but I believe that by repeating a treatment you are showing the chakras what it is like to be in a state of balance, and that repeated exposure to this balanced state, by providing a series of treatments, helps to move the recipient's chakras more into a state of balance long-term.

Another challenge to the 'Reiki is perfectly intelligent, we do not need to develop ourselves as a channel, we do not need to work intuitively" point of view is the fact that people are able to develop an intuitive ability and find that their hands are guided into combinations of hand positions that are different from one person to another, and different from one treatment to another.

This suggests, of course, that there are sequences of hand positions that are more appropriate or effective in dealing with an individual's problems on that occasion than simply applying a standard template.

If a standard template is always sufficient – or just holding someone's hands for an hour is all that is needed – why would our hands be guided by the energy to direct the energy into particular areas, distinctive for that recipient and different from the hand positions elicited for another person?

Intuitive working

In practice, I have found that people treated with intuitively-guided hand positions find that the energy seems to penetrate more deeply, that the treatments feel in some way more relevant, more profound, more effective than when standard positions are used, and that is my impression too.

Treatments based on intuitively-guided hand positions seem more powerful, sometimes a lot more powerful, than treatments based on standard hand positions, since we are directing the energy into just the right combination, and sequence, of positions for that person on that occasion.

If we look to the origins of Reiki and the way that Mikao Usui taught, we can see that intuitive working was a fundamental part of the practice of Reiki, and still is in Mikao Usui's Reiki Association in Japan to this day.

Why would Usui have placed so much emphasis on using intuition if standard hand positions - or no hand positions - are just as good in terms of producing good results? He was a practical man, after all. So there is something special about working intuitively: it seems to do more than standard hand positions can.

Hand positions for different ailments

For the benefit of students who could not yet work intuitively (and that is the important point), Chujiro Hayashi produced a long list of what could be described as 'good places to put your hands for different medical conditions', which suggests that certain combinations of hand positions are more effective in dealing with specific conditions that applying a standard template.

Why would Dr Hayashi have produced such a list if, as many believe, Reiki is an intelligent energy that always goes where it is needed? We should remember, though, that this list was a stopgap, and that intuitive working was the ideal.

The above suggests that although Reiki may be intelligent to an extent – or the recipient's body is intelligent to an extent – we can enhance our treatments through some of the things that we can do, for example allowing the energy to guide us in terms of where we place our hands.

Further inconsistencies in the 'Reiki is perfectly intelligent' point of view come through the use of symbols: if we think about it, as soon as we start using any of the Reiki symbols in the Western fashion, perhaps routinely drawing the symbols as we treat, in a pre-determined sequence, we are consciously over-riding the way that the energy wants to work when left to its own devices, and imposing our will by directing the energy in a certain way.

Yet if the energy knows exactly what to and where to go, why would we need to use symbols? Why would we need to impose our control over the energy in this way?

But this is not the only way that the symbols can be used. Just in the same way that we can move beyond standard hand positions to embrace intuitive working, with all the benefits that are associated with this, we can also work intuitively when we use the symbols, allowing the energy to guide us in terms of which aspect of the energy we emphasise, if any, during a treatment. Thus we work in partnership with the energy.

I believe that Reiki is an intelligent energy to an extent, and is drawn by the recipient's need to the appropriate areas, sometimes over-riding the way that we have directed the energy if that is required.

However, we can assist in providing just what the recipient needs on each occasion by working intuitively, by being open and allowing the energy to guide us.

I believe that we work in partnership with the energy, and that we are not simply empty tubes through which the energy flows.

Through the development of our intuition, we can understand how the energy needs to be directed by us to better help our clients: where best to put our hands, and what aspects of the energy need to be emphasised.

About the Author

Taggart King is a Reiki Master Teacher, Cognitive Hypnotherapist and NLP Master Practitioner who has been teaching Japanese-style Reiki through live and then home study courses for over 20 years.

He founded Reiki Evolution in 1998.

Taggart has written eight books about Reiki, created several Reiki-related journals and recorded a dozen audio collections (on CD and MP3) comprising guided meditations and audio commentary to accompany all the Reiki levels and practices.

Reiki Evolution

Reiki Evolution offers small-scale Reiki courses through a team of 'trusted teachers' in the UK, all of whom offer Taggart's style of Reiki courses. There are never more than 4-6 students on any course so we can give you individual attention.

And finally, Taggart teaches Reiki mainly through home study courses.

Cognitive Hypnotherapy

Taggart qualified as a Cognitive Hypnotherapist in 2010, and as a NLP Master Practitioner, with The Quest Institute, training with its founder, Trevor Silvester.

He has also assisted in the training of new students on the Quest Diploma and NLP Master Practitioner courses.

Printed in Great Britain
by Amazon